7ª   39ſ

8(1264|

D1451683

The Biblical Web

The Biblical Web

Ruth apRoberts

Ann Arbor

The University of Michigan Press

Copyright © by the University of Michigan 1994
All rights reserved
Published in the United States of America by
The University of Michigan Press
Manufactured in the United States of America
⊛ Printed on acid-free paper
1997   1996   1995   1994   4   3   2   1

A CIP catalogue record for this book is available from the British Library.

Library of Congress Cataloging-in-Publication Data
ApRoberts, Ruth.
    The Biblical web / Ruth apRoberts.
      p.   cm.
    Includes bibliographical references and index.
    ISBN 0-472-10494-2 (alk. paper)
    1. Bible and literature. 2. Bible—Influence. 3. Bible—
Influence—Western civilization.   I. Title.
PN56.B5A67   1994
809'.93382—dc20   94-782
                                          CIP

Introductory Note

As the terms "Old Testament" and "New Testament" can be seen to represent a pro-Christian bias, I use "Hebrew Bible" and "Christian Bible," or HB and CB. There is some loss of logic in this, however, because for Christians, the "Bible" is both books. But I think it will be clear from context that CB here comprises the canonical Christian books written after the time of Jesus, of which the originals are in Greek. By the same logic, I use for dating "Before the Common Era" and "Common Era," or BCE and CE, instead of BC and AD. Other abbreviations used are KJV for the King James Version (in England the Authorized Version), RSV for Revised Standard Version, NEB for New English Bible, NIV for New International Version, and PB for Prayer Book (the Anglican Book of Common Prayer). For the KJV quotations I follow the translators' practice of italicizing verbal elements not in the original.

Contents

Chapter 1

Filaments

Nothing will be restrained from them
which they have imagined to do.

"Only connect," said E. M. Forster, and oh, we have, we have! How
little the various writers of the Bible could have expected that their
words would become part of life ages hence in the remote islands off
the far coasts of Europe, beyond Tarshish! Or how astounded the first
missionaries would have been to see how far "the light unto the
gentiles" had extended, at times not quite in the way they would
have expected. There is a yearning to connect one's own place with
important events of the Near East, and myths of visitation have
arisen to make the connection. France, Spain, India, and England all
have notable stories of visits by personages of the Christian Bible,
but the English tradition of the visit of Joseph of Arimathea, bringing
with him the Holy Grail, is particularly persistent, and elaborately
developed, being wound in with the whole complex of the national
Arthurian legend. Joseph is said, moreover, to have founded at
Glastonbury an English Church predating that of Rome. It has suited
some British to believe also that the Stone of Scone, on which English
monarchs are crowned, is the selfsame stone of the altar of the patri-
arch Jacob, brought from Bethel. And so the connection goes back
even to a text long predating the Christian Bible.

This stone from Bethel symbolizes the strong sense that comes
on us at times of the continuity of culture, ultimately of the linking
of all humanity, and this sense challenges our powers of expression.
Carlyle expressed it with a figure of "organic filaments," weaving
"the immeasurable, universal world-tissue," binding us together
both synchronically and diachronically, as we say now; or as he said:
"If now an existing generation of men stand so woven together, not
less indissolubly does generation with generation." His Professor

Teufelsdröckh's philosophy of clothes connects ultimately back, by an organic filament, to Cadmus of Thebes with his heroic gift of the alphabet, and to Gutenberg with his heroic gift of print. But even without the written message, "the heroic heart, the seeing eye of the first times, still feels and sees in us of the latest; . . . the Wise Man stands ever encompassed, and spiritually embraced, by a cloud of witnesses and brothers; and there is a living literal communion of Saints, wide as the World itself, and as the History of the World."[1] The filaments are infinitely interwoven. We speak, Carlyle says, of a "chain of causes," but it is rather "a tissue, or superficies of innumerable lines, extending in breadth as well as in length, and with a complexity which will foil and utterly bewilder the most assiduous computation."[2] Carlyle insists that of all filament systems the one of written words is the most potent, and wears the best. The others, "compared with this rich and boundless one of Literature . . . are poor, limited and ineffectual."[3] Temporal power, he insists, is in comparison ephemeral: now, Tamburlaine is as nothing to Gutenberg; now, Napoleon is as nothing to Goethe. "Literature" in this sense is not a fine or decorative art, and not for nothing is it originally sacred, holy scriptures.

Ancient Jewish culture had preeminently this sense of the holiness of language. From Genesis on, the *word* is numinous and powerful. *Naming* things is an element of God's act of creation, and man's similar power is recognized in Adam: "whatsoever Adam called every living creature, that was the name thereof" (Gen. 2:19). The account of the Tower of Babel is itself the best witness to language as power. When people understand each other's language "nothing will be restrained from them which they have imagined to do" (Gen. 11:6) and God is obliged to intervene, to break this god-rivaling power. The word once uttered can never be recalled, as in Jacob's fraudulent obtaining of the father's blessing, or Jephthah's tragic sacrifice of his daughter. The act of writing is still more sacred. The finger of God himself originally wrote the Tablets of the Law, and "The Lord said unto Moses, Write this for a memorial in a book." The Torah, the Law, is barely existent until Moses performs the sacred office of writing it. And to be "blotted out" of God's book is to be nonexistent. Isaiah admonishes his hearers: "Now go, write it before them in a table, and note it in a book, that it may be for the time to come for ever and ever: That this is a rebellious people . . . " (30:8–

9). Job, exasperated with his friends' false "comfort," cries out, "Oh that my words were now written! oh that they were printed in a book!" (19:23). (It is to our great advantage that indeed they have been, and stand printed before us.) And the reading from the *book* is essential in both Hebrew and Christian history.

It is to this sense of the holiness of the written word that we owe the treasure of the Bible, in innumerable languages and cultures. We have impiously defied the inhibition laid down at Babel, and the Bible has become of all texts unquestionably the most widely disseminated. The semioticians speak of all sorts of sign systems, including all "patterned" communication as well as language: mathematics, Morse code, music notation, chemical formulae, dance, psychoanalysis, cinema. But as Carlyle knew, the verbal, written system carries an enormous advantage over the nonverbal. The great pyramids of the Egyptians have survived *against* all likelihood, against both natural and human forces, both "sluttish time" and "wasteful war," which have had the victory in most cases. And the pyramids impress in good measure by their foreignness and mysteriousness. But Psalm 104 is generally thought to be Egyptian in origin and conceptions, about contemporary with the pyramids, coming to us through Egyptian, Canaanite, and Hebrew versions, later having been compared with Greek and Latin versions, and in the case of the KJV with German as well, and Wycliffe's version, and Cranmer's, and Tyndale's, and the Psalm is fresh, intelligible, immediate and our own. Unlike the crumbling sphinx, the psalm seems irrepressible. And so it is that these organic filaments have connected that very ancient time with our own. Probably no texts have been so well preserved so long.

Roland Barthes was full of the joy of the text. He declared that the confusion of languages is no longer a punishment; in the cohabitation of languages we live in *jouissance*, in this *Babel heureuse*.[4] The text is "completely woven with quotations, references, and echoes. These are cultural languages . . . past or present, that traverse the text from one end to the other in a vast stereophony."[5] And so Barthes speaks of *intertextuality*, and the impossibility of living outside of the "infinite text." "*Texte* veut dire *Tissu*," he says; *text* means *cloth*. "But this cloth is not a finished product, not a sort of veil behind which, more or less hidden, the meaning (the truth) lies hidden; we insist rather on the generative idea which the text makes itself, working across a perpetual interlacing . . . in this cloth, this texture. . . . "[6]

And he proposes a name for the theory of the text: *hyphology,* for *hyphos,* "c'est le tissu et la toile d'araignée." In different languages, we can do different things which we imagine to do, and it was a little hard in French to maintain the metaphor of *l'araignée,* the spider. Spiders don't have a positive image in French,[7] and the French have to say *tissu* or *toile*—*fabric* or *cloth*—where we can say *web.* Of course the spider can be rather negative: we can be caught and victimized by the web of meanings; but on the whole *web* has caught on in English and has been taken up with satisfaction by anglophone semioticians. An introduction to Semiotics speaks of this "vast semiotic web" and quotes Cassirer on how human beings "weave the symbolic net, the tangled web of human experience."[8] The semioticians remind us that language itself "provides the collective with a presumption of communicability," and they see the written record as the "patrimony of human collectivity."[9] And the magisterial series of annuals edited by the Sebeoks is called *The Semiotic Web.*[10] How interesting that early on Carlyle anticipated this with his "organic filaments" and "the immeasurable World-tissue"; and likewise that his philosophy of clothes anticipates the cultural anthropologist. We can see culture now as a vast "web of semiosis, a thick tapestry of interwoven sign systems."[11]

Since the Bible is probably the longest-lived of all texts, the most translated, the most widely disseminated, it might seem to offer the most challenging field for the study of intertextuality, for this interweaving and interlacing, and I here present some studies of strands, or sets of strands, that have interwoven themselves particularly in English-speaking culture, and in sympathy with the semioticists have called this book *The Biblical Web.* The web is made up of organic filaments stretching from about 3000 BCE to now, uniting those writers of words of so long ago into a communion with ourselves.

The mere transportation of an altar stone from Bethel to Westminster is really less marvelous (and less true) than the appropriation of the Bible itself by translation into English. The story of the translation is a sort of national epic in its own right, with its heroes and martyrs of Protestant ideology, from King Alfred, to Wycliffe and his contraband Bible, to Tyndale, the main shaper of the English biblical idiom, who died at the stake, a martyr to translation, to the great committee set up by King James, comprised of the best scholars and best stylists at a time when England excelled in scholarship and litera-

ture. Even the one other great vernacular Bible, Luther's, contributed
to the excellence of the KJV, for Tyndale in exile was closely associated with the Lutherans and borrowed much of the power and sim-
plicity of Luther's version for his own.[12]

From early times, there seems to have been a great English relish
for the Hebrew Bible despite its official demotion by the Christian
message. While it would be a false simplification and distortion of
theology to say that the Roman Catholic continent favors the CB and
the Protestants the HB, there is recurrently something of a difference
in emphasis. Tyndale's enthusiasm for Hebrew as a language that
translates well into English suggests a sense of affinity. The Hebrew
language, he exclaims with charming enthusiasm, agrees with English "a thousand times more" than Greek or Latin.[13] And when the
King's Committee came to revise and adapt Tyndale, they seem to
have preserved the Hebraic vigor that Tyndale had such feeling for.
By the time of Cromwell, the Puritans took on a passionate identification with HB history and felt themselves to be Israelites once more
fighting the battles against the enemies of Jehovah. The Puritans
opposing the monarchists and Catholics could refer to Samuel's mis-
givings and warnings against kings; the Cavaliers on the other hand
could lean on promonarchical texts as supporting the Divine Right
of kings. "Long live the King" is a line out of the KJV HB, and British
monarchs are anointed with oil by the Archbishop of Canterbury just
as Saul and David were by Samuel.

It was a Puritan who first promulgated the peculiar theory that
the English and their kin are descended from the "Lost Ten Tribes"
of Israel that were taken captive into Assyria in 721 BCE and thereafter
disappeared from Hebrew history. How they got to England is told
in very creative historical vein, and kooky linguistic evidence is
brought to bear: *Britons* are originally *Berit-Ish* in Hebrew, and *Saxons*
are clearly *Isaac's sons*, and so on.[14] The movement became strong in
the eighteenth century and contributed to Blake's visions of Albion
as Israel. It continued through the nineteenth century as the "British
Israel World Federation," with many exotic appendages; passages
through the Great Pyramid at Giza, for instance, are an allegory of
world history that predicts the primacy of the British Empire. Insofar
as the British have felt "chosen" they could identify comfortably with
the original "chosen people," if not to be "a light unto the gentiles"
at least the bearer of the white man's burden.

It was the greatest Puritan of them all who made the greatest domestication of biblical material. In *Samson Agonistes* Milton engrafts classical form on HB material to produce the most perfect "Greek" tragedy in English. With true Protestant freedom of interpretation, he has the audacity to convert the mindless strong man of the Bible into a classical hero. The still more astounding audacity of the man in undertaking to amalgamate the Bible with the classical tradition of the epic is quite as wonderful as the magnificent achievement itself. Milton read Hebrew and Syriac and Greek and did not have to depend on English translations. However, he carefully eschewed anyway the royalist Anglican KJV in favor of the Geneva English Bible (1560), and the Roman Catholic Vulgate in favor of the Tremellius Protestant Latin Version (1579). In *Samson Agonistes* and *Paradise Lost* Milton established an English mode of the exploitation and elaboration of Hebrew material—according, of course, to Christian theology. But the cultural high points on the continent are grounded in the CB: Dante's *Divine Comedy* in Scholasticism and Thomist Catholicism, Bach's great masses and passions in liturgy and the gospels. When after *Paradise Lost* Milton turns to the CB for his sequel, *Paradise Regained*, the result is pale and anticlimactic. It seems that the English genius finds special inspiration and relevance in the HB.

The Puritan identification with the Israelites extended with a vengeance into the New World. American place-names suggest the pathos with which the Puritans sought refuge as sojourners in a strange land: There are nine Goshens in the United States, also twelve Bethels, five Zions or Sions, four Carmels, two each of Ramah, Mizpah, Shiloh, Bethesda, and no less than eighteen Salems. Other countries simply do not show this predilection. South Africa has one Goshen, New Zealand has a Jerusalem, and that's about it. But in America, the Bible supplied the place-names and shaped the psyche, as has been well demonstrated in American literary studies,[15] and the Bible still stays current. Look, for instance, at what is probably the best known song in the whole country, "The Battle Hymn of the Republic":

Mine eyes have seen the glory of the coming of the Lord:
He is trampling out the vintage where the grapes of wrath are
                                                    stored.

The imagery is taken from the book of Isaiah. Before Julia Ward Howe composed the words, William Lloyd Garrison had denounced slavery in the words of Isaiah, as "a covenant with death and an agreement with hell,"[16] and when she came to write her mind was full of such abolitionist rhetoric and the Hebrew imagery current in the pulpits. The winepress image is of a very ancient provenance; it was already old when the Deutero-Isaiah came to write: long ago, Jacob, in his deathbed predictions for his twelve sons, prophesies prosperity for Judah. Wine will be so plentiful that it will be used for laundry: "he washed his garments in wine, and his clothes in the blood of grapes."[17] It is a fairly obvious metaphor, wine as the *blood* of grapes (so long as it is not a question of white wine). It certainly suggests an extravagant (if inefficient) lifestyle. But Isaiah develops the metaphor with virtuosity for the theme of divine retribution: God is the treader of the winepress, and the wine is the blood of the wicked:

> Who is this that cometh from Edom,
> with dyed garments from Bozrah?
> This *that is* glorious in his apparel,
> travelling in the greatness of his strength?
> I that speak in righteousness,
> Mighty to save.
> Wherefore *art thou* red in thine apparel,
> and thy garments like him that treadeth in the winefat?
> I have trodden the winepress alone;
> and of the people *there was* none with me:
> for I will tread them in mine anger,
> and trample them in my fury;
> and their blood shall be sprinkled upon my garments,
> and I will stain all my raiment.
>
> . . . .
> And I will tread down the people in mine anger,
> and make them drunk in my fury,
> and I will bring down their strength to the earth.
>
> (Isa. 63:1–6)

The situation is that the Lord to avenge his people is treading down the enemy, Edom, and the enemy's city, Bozrah (near Amman, Jordan). The specifics might not matter much to the nineteenth-century reader, for the point is clear enough: the day of reckoning is at hand. Jeremiah too uses the figure:

> For thus saith the Lord God of Israel unto me;
> Take the wine cup of this fury at my hand
> and cause all the nations, to whom I send thee,
> to drink it.
>
> (Jer. 25:15)

And Joel, thought to be later, postexilic, would seem to develop it still further:

> Put ye in the sickle, for the harvest is ripe:
> come, get you down; for the press is full,
> the fats [wine-vats] overflow; for their wickedness is great.
> Multitudes, multitudes in the valley of decision:
> for the day of the Lord *is* near in the valley of decision.[18]
>
> (Joel 3:13–14)

The writer of Revelation, very familiar with the prophets, is much later ringing changes on the same figure:

> . . . Babylon is fallen . . . because she made all nations
> drink of the wine of the wrath of her fornication. . . .
> drink of the wine of the wrath of God. . . .
> Gather the clusters of the wine of the earth;
> for her grapes are fully ripe. . . .
> And the angel thrust his sickle into the earth,
> and cast it into the great winepress of the wrath of God.
> And the winepress was trodden without the city,
> and blood came out of the winepress.
>
> (Rev. 14:8–20)

In chapter 15, the seven plagues are called the "seven bowls of God's wrath." And in chapter 19, the apocalyptic figure of Christ appears and "treadeth the winepress of the fierceness and wrath of Almighty God." Such were the lurid images that fired the abolitionist crusade and enforced the sense of the Civil War as a day of reckoning, a reckoning to be paid in blood.[19]

Oddly enough, another civil war had brought on the same turn for exploiting such imagery—England's seventeenth-century civil war. The young historian Thomas Babington Macaulay, recreating the battles of that time, wrote two "Songs of the Civil War," one "The Cavalier's March to London" that is full of aristocratic bluster, and the other, the Roundhead's song that is passionately felt: "The Battle of Naseby, by Obadiah-Bind-Their-Kings-In-Chains-And-Their-Nobles-With-Links-Of-Iron, Sergeant in Ireton's Regiment." Perhaps there never was a time when the Bible was more in men's speech than with the Puritans, even in their names, as Macaulay with evident delight records (his singer's name may or may not be authentic; it is from Psalm 149:8, PB version). And this Puritan song begins:

Oh! wherefore come ye forth, in triumph from the North,
With your hands, and your feet, and your raiment all red?
And wherefore doth your rout send forth a joyous shout?
And whence be the grapes of the wine-press which ye tread?

Oh, evil was the root, and bitter was the fruit,
And crimson was the juice of the vintage that we trod;
For we trampled on the throng of the haughty and the strong,
Who sat in the high places, and slew the saints of God.[20]

It is perfectly clear that Howe and Macaulay are drawing on the same passage from Isaiah. Macaulay's poem may have been in Howe's memory—conscious or unconscious. (She does not mention him in her *Reminiscences*.)[21] We have before us at any rate the range of source elements—and it seems to me to be clear, and much to her credit, that she originated, so far as I know, the actual phrase the "grapes of wrath." John Steinbeck borrowed some of its power for the title of his novel, full of a passionate sense of social retribution. The Battle Hymn exploits and reactivates a powerful passage from Isaiah with a resonance of its own that still affects us. We feel obliged, still, to anticipate days of reckoning. This theme of winepress is just one example of the many strands of that great "web of semiosis" stretching from ancient time to now.[22]

Virtually all writers of English draw on the Bible, and the more memorable ones are the great recyclers of biblical elements. Imagine Shakespeare, for instance, reading his Geneva Bible. It, like the early editions of the KJV, included the Apocrypha, which are too little read these days. He and his Shylock well knew the clever story of Susanna and Daniel's legal skill ("A Daniel come to judgment!"). I think he knew also the beautiful apocryphal Wisdom of Solomon. The writer speaks of the sufferings of the Egyptians under the plagues: "their grief was double with mourning and the remembrance of things past."[23] And so,

> When to the sessions of sweet silent thought
> I summon up remembrance of things past . . . ,

it seems to me that the little phrase is just distinctive enough, with its reversal of normal word order, to have stood in Shakespeare's file of memory, ready to be summoned up for a space of six syllables, two iambs and a heavy, ruminative spondee. From Shakespeare's memorable sonnet it stayed with Scott Moncrieff and popped up when he came to seek a title for his translation of Proust's *À la recherche du temps perdu,* although it is hardly accurate as a translation.[24] But it satisfied the urge we have to borrow some aura of Shakespeare or the Bible to give our book titles distinction. Borrow a little sanctified resonance and it will rub off on your book. So once more the phrase was renewed in the English tradition. When the Anchor Bible translates it as "memories of things bygone," it seems a gratuitous and pointless change for the sake of change.[25] Perhaps, however, the Anchor translator wants to avoid precisely that aura of literariness that has overlaid the text.

A famous line from Ecclesiastes gives us another nicely exemplary strand of this biblical web of meanings: "Vanity of vanities, saith the Preacher, vanity of vanities; all *is* vanity." "Preacher" translates the Hebrew "Koheleth," and nobody knows who that is or what it means. The rest of the Hebrew is clear, though: Hebrew doesn't have the superlative and resorts to a common Near Eastern idiom as in "King of Kings" or "Holy of holies," and here it is a word for *breath* or *vapor*—"vapor of vapors," then. "Breath of a breath" the Anchor has it,[26] "the slightest breath! All is a breath!" Or as the NEB puts it, "Emptiness, emptiness, says the Speaker, all is empty." The

NIV Interlinear Hebrew-English version, more or less obliged to verbal exactness, translates it "Meaninglessness of meaninglessnesses, says the Teacher, meaninglessness of meaninglessnesses, the whole meaninglessness." One feels somehow one should tell them these versions will never catch on. Both NEB and Interlinear have deleted the typically Hebrew metaphor: The Hebrew writer took *breath* as a vivid way of saying *emptiness* or *meaninglessness*—or fleetingness or insubstantiality or nothingness. Jerome (or some predecessor in Latin) also rejects the metaphor but takes the convenient Latin word for *empty, vanus,* and writes "Vanitas vanitatum," which preserves the Hebrew idiom if not the metaphor. It runs through the book like a refrain. It runs also down through the years in English culture. The peculiar antireligious or absurdist elements of the book melt away under ingenious religious exegesis, and by the fourteenth century *vanity* has become firmly associated with worldly things as opposed to spiritual, in all Europe. In the Piazza della Signoria in Florence in 1497, inspired by Savonarola, the people gathered together all the appurtenances of this worldliness—masks, wigs, cosmetics, licentious books and pictures—into a great apocryphal cleansing fire, called "the burning of vanities." Savonarola's bonfire becomes George Eliot's subject in her novel *Romola* (1863). In Chaucer, vanity is associated with a great fair as metaphor for the world:

> O yonge fresshe folkes, he or she,
> In which that love up groweth with youre age,
> Repeyreth hom fro worldly vanyte,
>
> . . . .
> . . . and thynketh al nys but a faire
> This world, that passeth soone as floures faire.[27]

John Bunyan picks up the cue and envisions "Vanity Fair" as that place where his hero Christian is much impeded and delayed on his journey to salvation. This wonderful figure is all the more full of moral import for the vividness of its realism: the old-fashioned country fair with all its fairings—food, drink, luxury, sex—all as beautifully varied as the Seven Deadly Sins to keep us in all manner of dereliction from the straight and narrow. Thackeray in an inspired moment chose it for the title of his sorry human spectacle of all sorts of people moving about to gratify their urges and egos. Even his "good" people are culpable, Amelia for her vanity of stubborn blindness, Dobbin for his of over-meekness. The figure of speech continues so effective that a magazine *Vanity Fair* was established to celebrate the pleasures of this world, and even now in these latter days has been revived, with a kind of smart sophisticated writing about the Beautiful People and their beautiful concerns. And now Tom Wolfe, in a novel exploring the ingenious ubiquitous inventiveness of evil, calls his work, with a glance toward Savonarola, *The Bonfire of the Vanities*. The novel is a kind of incineration.

As these varied examples may suggest, the present book is a study in the continuity of culture, biblical culture, not through mere centuries but through something like eons. The motive behind the dissemination of the Bible has been primarily religious, though at times political, and it has occasioned what is unquestionably the largest translation operation in all history, into thousands of languages, in a plethora of versions at times even in the same language. The bibliography of versions in English alone is enormous. It is a pleasant irony that the book that recounts the disaster at Babel is the occasion of this vast contra-Babel project. Even now the Gideons put Bibles in our hotel rooms, and religious organizations underwrite the new translations into yet more languages that appear every year. Protestant societies, with their emphasis on the Bible as the sole rule of faith and on the power of individuals to interpret for themselves, are naturally more given to biblical translation, and the two best translations are generally granted to be Luther's German one and the KJV, the one due to a great leader who was also a great literary man, the other a collaborative product of a body of great writers, the sole example, it has been said, of great work done by a committee.

English-speaking culture is imbued, in its idiom and its literature, with the writings of Shakespeare; and it is likewise imbued—but even more so—with the Bible, because the Bible was very familiar for religious reasons. But it is also familiar for the same reasons that Shakespeare is familiar: because these English texts are full of memorable people and events and psychological states, and supremely memorable language. There is the religious impulse, that is; but over and beyond that there is, if one may say so, the literary impulse. There are those that disdain "the Bible as Literature,"[28] but especially since the nineteenth century there has been a trend toward literary analysis, impeded at times by conscious or unconscious sectarian views and troubled at times by doctrinal issues, but still laboring toward just analysis and interpretation; and there has been lately a great expansion of this secular biblical scholarship. Robert Alter and Frank Kermode in the Introduction to their recent *Literary Guide to the Bible* write of the "revival of interest in the literary qualities of these texts. . . . " There is now available "a new view of the Bible as a work of great literary force and authority, a work of which it is entirely credible that it should have shaped the minds and lives of intelligent men and women for two millennia and more." We neglect it to "our immense cost."[29] The principle of this kind of study is that literary historical analysis must take precedence. A time-honored or sacred mistranslation must be known for what it is. "I know that my redeemer liveth" is not, cannot be, a statement of Christian faith, for it is in fact Job speaking within the framework of Near Eastern law court conventions. Nor, scholars agree, can Isaiah's "Behold, a virgin shall conceive" predict the miraculous birth of Jesus, because, for one thing, the Hebrew word does not mean "virgin." Of course there are time-honored mistakes that have contributed in notable ways to culture, like Jerome's mistaken description of Moses coming down from Sinai with *horns* on his head. The approved translation of an acknowledgedly difficult Hebrew word is *rays of light*. But in the meantime we have a long iconographic tradition of the horned Moses, of which Michelangelo's statue is the most famous example. Such mistakes make an interesting study in themselves. But the project of literary analysis is to discover meaning as best we can, avoiding all the mistakes we can, and the exegete who neglects literary analysis neglects meaning. It may be at last that literary analysis will enrich the religious understanding of the text, but meantime, in this book, religious questions are deferred.

The essays here, then, put doctrine aside and trace some of the broader social, cultural, and literary effects of the Bible in English, chiefly the King James Version. Like all translations, the English version makes the Bible appear much more monolithic than it is in the languages of the originals, which vary from the earliest known Hebrew to Hebrew of about 300 BCE, showing linguistic changes about as great as from Anglo-Saxon to modern English; furthermore, in later HB texts some passages are in Aramaic, the Semitic language which was the vernacular in Palestine in the time of Jesus; and then the books of the CB are translated, not from the Aramaic Jesus spoke, but from the demotic street Greek or *koine* of the first century. And so the Bible appears before us much more as an entity than as a library of *biblia*, the Greek plural "books," from which our word Bible comes. The KJV is pretty uniformly the English of 1611 (or a little earlier—the Committee did little to update current English versions that were already established). It is a learned and composite text showing cognizance of many versions including the Greek Septuagint, Jerome's and other Latin versions, even—through Tyndale—Luther's German. The translators conscientiously and meticulously indicate elements they have interpolated for smoothness of reading, by setting them in italics—no other vernacular Bible does this, I believe.

The first essay in the book takes up the translation of Hebrew poetry. I had been struck by the fact that most literary studies of biblical texts centered on prose narrative, which is a comparatively unproblematic kind of translation, given that all translations must necessarily change the original and that lexical choices must skew meanings. But poetry is notoriously untranslatable; it has even been wittily defined as what does not translate. However, I argue that because of its peculiar structure according to semantics not phonics, Hebrew poetry is remarkably translatable, and has been indeed remarkably well translated. Hence it has entered the cultural mainstream as few other translated texts have.

In the essay "The Multiplication of Similitudes," I have studied another aspect of this translatableness: metaphor. Hebrew poetry is highly metaphorical, and the metaphors are mostly such as are intelligible to a broad range of cultures. Most of us have been impressed by the beauty and power of the wings of an eagle, and to be borne up by God "as on eagle's wings" is a very readily apprehensible image—of power, of nobility, of strength, of transcendence. To try to explain the figure without metaphor is to be dull and inapprehensible. Or take the so easily translatable metaphor of the shepherd and his flock: how rich and dense and generative it is as it runs through European literature and art.

Another essay, "Waiting for Gödel," studies how the literary manipulation of perspective in the book of Job set a precedent for, and possibly influenced, literary insights that have a respectable analogue in philosophy and make a difficult philosophical concept conceivable. In general, it is the triumph of these texts to make difficult or remote notions assimilable which would not have been so in discursive prose.

Next there is a study of the text of Handel's *Messiah*, the English oratorio by the German who became the most English of composers. As it is probably the most widely disseminated anthology of English biblical verses in all English-speaking culture, it is time to give it the literary analysis it might be expected to deserve. Following this is a study of Robert Lowth, Handel's younger contemporary and the greatest of English biblical critics. His exposition of the parallel structure of Hebrew poetry illuminated the field immeasurably, his appreciation of biblical metaphor was radically forward-looking, his translation of Isaiah demonstrated the value of the literary approach, and his work in general gave impetus to the German school of Higher Criticism and to the Romantic movement in literature.

Finally, there is an essay on some Victorian phenomena that keep biblical culture current: Matthew Arnold's schoolbook edition of Isaiah, and the poetic recycling of biblical texts by poets at opposite poles of thought—A. E. Housman the atheist and G. M. Hopkins the Jesuit. These are all only samples of this biblical survival, which may perhaps lead the reader to a further awareness of how it still continues. They are instances of the prevalence of this extraordinarily influential strain of writings that developed and were collected in the small area of the world that stretches from the Nile to Mount Ararat, the "fertile crescent," that remains even more fertile culturally than agriculturally. And the English-speaking peoples, because of their Protestant Bible-reading history, because of the concatenation of literary-historical forces that made the English version particularly potent, and sometimes because of a sense of cultural superiority that persuaded the English they were the Lost Tribes of Israel and that Jesus walked in England's green and pleasant land, appropriated these texts in particularly dynamic ways. It is probably the longest cultural continuity in the history of humankind. "I have considered the days of old, the years of ancient time," said the Psalmist (77:5); and we can do so too, and trace and revere those filaments that bind us to the days of old, and so immensely enrich the heritage of community. This heritage, moreover, is by no means static; we engage with it in dialogue and infinite transformation. "We live in traditions," says Gadamer, and these are not a fragment of our world-experience, not a matter of "cultural transmissions" emerging from texts and monuments and communicating a meaning that is linguistically composed and historically documented. Rather, it is the world itself that is communicatively experienced and constantly given over to us as an infinitely open task.[30]

Chapter 2

Hebrew Poetry: The Translatable Structure

Translation is notoriously impossible, but this does not deter people from doing it.[1] And, of course, we cannot do without it. We have never really accepted the destruction of the Tower of Babel and—recalcitrant and impious—keep trying to put some of the pieces together. God is conceived as knowing that language is power: "Behold, the people *is* one, and they have all one language . . . and now nothing will be restrained from them which they have imagined to do."[2] If we could understand all the languages, we might become godlike in our ecumenicism and interdisciplinary powers, but in the meantime, having some few powers of translation, we can do some few of the things "that we have imagined to do." George Steiner in *After Babel* argues for a new legitimacy to be granted to our efforts, to the process of translation. Communication is never perfect, even in one language; translation from one language to another would appear to be, then, only a degree less of perfection. Our hearing, reading, and understanding are all a kind of translation. To be human, Steiner suggests, is to paraphrase, to translate. Jeremy Bentham conceived that language itself, in its fictive, nonabsolute quality, is "impossible but indispensable"; we might apply this to translation, to corroborate Steiner. We do not accept the impossible as such. Steiner observes that just as the Fall is interpreted as the *felix culpa*, having within it the possibility of the Redeemer, so does that "disaster at Babel" have in it "the movement towards and beyond Pentecost."[3] The poet W. H. Auden has seen the gift of tongues in a somewhat similar way: "The pentecostal marvel, where each in each finds his right translator" ("Ode to Terminus"). And in fact, our punishment by multiplicities of languages, our terrible failure to understand each other, is a very ambiguous punishment, felicitous in that we are immeasurably enriched by the fullness and variety of words and grammars in the world. Theologians consider us the richer spiritually for the multiplicity of names for deity.[4] The secular Horace celebrates his Lydia as *multi nominis;* the beloved has many names.

In spite of the punitive occasion of the destruction of the Tower, it is, paradoxically, through a great fullness of translations that the occasion and its context are widely known. The Bible must be the most widely translated of all documents. It must then afford the richest field for the study of translations, and I want to consider here a special and peculiarly successful part of this translating enterprise: the poetry of the Hebrew Bible. The peculiarity of the success is of considerable interest for itself: it is generally granted that poetry is much more untranslatable than prose. In fact, it is common to define poetry as "what does not translate." And always this must be true, to a degree. The language of the poem must be the thing in itself. We know, with Carlyle, that "Language is called the Garment of Thought; however, it should rather be, Language is the Flesh-Garment, the Body, of Thought."[5] And because the language is somehow more the body in poetry, we do accept prose in translation more easily and even feel we may exercise the craft of criticism on novels we know only in translation, where we would not touch poetry in translation.

Obviously, one main reason for the "untranslatableness" of poetry is its formal qualities. It is more patterned than prose. And this form or pattern is typically of sounds: rhyme, rhythm, accent, alliteration, quantity, line length, stanza length, and so on. But the Hebrew poetry of the HB is not typical in this way. Unquestionably there are some elements of sound pattern in Hebrew verse; most certainly, paronomasia, or wordplay of the punning sort. But on other matters of sound pattern, learned opinion is much divided. Some scholars work out accent and alliteration patterns and syllable counts. But one, James Muilenburg, holds that the Hebrew poet deliberately eschews metrical consistency.[6] There is no question at all, however, that the supreme operational formal principle is a system of parallelism, of lines, or members, or *stichoi* as they are variously called; and also of parallelism within the lines, and less conspicuously of groups of lines in related clusters, with chiasmus frequent both in small units and in large, sometimes with refrains, and often with an *inclusio,* or a return at the end to the beginning, marking what is sometimes called ring structure.

Take first a passage from Judith. Although it is neither canonical nor classical, it conveniently displays the structural unit. Judith's ingenious and heroic action in the killing of Holofernes is celebrated in a triumphal song that includes this triplet:

> Her sandal ravished his eyes,
> Her beauty captured his mind,
> And the sword severed his neck.
>
> (Jth. 16:9 RSV)

There is here a linear time logic, whereas more typically in the Prophets and Psalms the members dilate and complement each other in a manner more synchronic than diachronic. But the consistency of elements is typical. The syntactical and grammatical parallelism is obvious—subject-noun, transitive verb, object-noun. Note further the symmetrical interplay of literal and figurative. The first line has the very successful and typical Hebraic synecdoche of literal *sandal* to represent her whole beautiful attire; *ravished,* the concrete verb used figuratively; and *eyes,* literal. The second line proceeds from abstract *beauty,* to concrete verb *captured* used figuratively, to *mind,* which is—let us say—abstract; though with Holofernes getting progressively stoned, presumably with a combination of barbiturates and alcohol, his mind is becoming progressively concrete. The third line dramatically forgoes metaphor, with the sensational concrete literalism of *sword-sever-neck.* The pattern then runs:

concrete-figurative	figurative	concrete-literal
abstract	figurative	abstract
concrete-literal	concrete-literal	concrete-literal

Moreover, there is, again typically, the suprasyntactical message: by force of the parallelism, it is as good as said that beauty was used as a weapon. This is in sum an effective piece of lyric verse, in the line of the great triumph songs of Miriam and of Deborah, and the essential effect is due not to sound patterns but to a sort of idea-rhyming.

To turn to greater poetry, the beginning of the prophecy of Isaiah:

The ox knoweth his owner	a_1
and the ass his master's crib	a_2
But Israel doth not know	b_1
my people doth not consider	b_2
Ah sinful nation	c_1
a people laden with iniquity	c_2
A seed of evildoers	d_1
children that are corruptors	d_2
They have forsaken the Lord	e_1
they have provoked the Holy One of Israel unto anger	e_2
they are gone away backward	e_3

$$(1:3-4)$$

These lines demonstrate conveniently another kind of meaning expansion, in patterns of "synonymous" parallelism. Synonyms of course are never identical, and the gradations among them here are beautiful in their progressions. *Ox* and *ass* are obviously stupid beasts, and the *ass* as stupider comes second: the ox *and even* the ass. Even these beasts know whom they belong to, but *Israel* (b_1), explained as *my people* (b_2) to indicate possession, first (b_1) are not even aware of their owner, and then (b_2) do not even give the matter a thought. Now it is clear that the Lord is our owner, and by "master's crib" (a_2), the feeding place, it is clear also that it is he who sustains us. Then there are two pairs of laments, c_1 basic, c_2 intensifying c_1 (*laden*); then the d pair take the evil as though ingrained, genetically, with *seed* and *children*. Then the rhetorically effective triplet states the dereliction in mutually explicatory terms in climactic order. Let us compare Jerome:

Cognovit bos possessorum suum	a_1
et asinus praesepe domini sui	a_2
Israel autem me non cognovit	b_1
et populus meus non intellexit	b_2

Vae genti peccatrici c_1
populo gravi iniquitate c_2

semini nequam d_1
filiis sceleratis d_2

dereliquerunt Dominum e_1
blasphemaverunt sanctum Israel e_2
abalienati sunt retrorsum e_3

Jerome preserves the niceties of the progression, ox to ass, *knowing* to a more sophisticated intellection, sinful to *heavy* with sin, seed and children, and then dereliction—not to *angering* God but *blaspheming* (which must be just about as bad), and then the reversal or going away from him. The Jerusalem French translation reads

La boeuf connaît son possesseur a_1
et l'âne la crèche de son maître a_2

Israel ne connaît pas b_1
mon peuple ne comprend pas b_2

Malheur! nation pécheresse! c_1
peuple coupable! c_2

race de malfaiteurs d_1
fils pervertis! d_2

Ils ont abandonné Yahvé e_1
ils ont meprisé le Saint d'Israel e_2
ils se sont detournés de lui. e_3

The French moves similarly, though *coupable* seems much weaker than *laden with sin*, *meprisé* weaker than either angering God or blaspheming, and *detournés* a weak turning away rather than going in the opposite direction. And as Luther puts it:

Eine Ochse kennt seinen Herrn a_1
und ein Esel die Krippe seines Herrn a_2

aber Israel kennt's nicht b_1
und mein Volk versteht's nicht b_2

Wehe dem sündigen Volk c_1
dem Volk mit Schuld beladen c_2

dem boshaften Geschlecht d_1
den verderbten Kindern d_2

die den Herrn verlassen e_1
den Heiligen Israels lästern e_2
die abgefallen sind! e_3

The German sustains the pattern vigorously, going with blaspheming (*lästern*) rather than angering; *abgefallen*, however, seems an almost technical abstraction for apostate, less vivid than the English going away *backward*. But it is very clear that the ideational rhyme of parallel members functions in all these versions, variable as they are according to linguistic and cultural variations. If one reads through the verses taking only one item from each set, how very weak and thin the result!—and how very much more vulnerable to mistranslation. For one more short example, take the couplet that opens Psalm 51:

Have mercy upon me, O God,
    according to thy lovingkindness:
    according to the multitude of thy tender mercies
blot out my transgressions. . . .

Here is a chiasm that can be diagrammed *a b b a*, just like the quatrain of a Petrarchan sonnet. Jerome and the French translation show the *a b b a*, but Luther, as it happens, has *a b a b*:

Gott, sei mir gnädig
    nach deiner Gute,
Und tilge meine Sünden
    nach deiner grossen Barmherzigkeit.

But even with such variation, these different versions consist of a couplet with matching parts, which rhyme in this special sense of *semantic* rhyme. And, in all, the meanings expand by virtue of the pattern: *thy lovingkindness* is as a *multitude of tender mercies*, and to *have mercy* is to *blot out transgressions*! Perhaps it can be seen, even from these small units, how eminently—even uniquely—translatable these verses are.

To appreciate this translatableness, it is interesting to turn back to the 1970s and salvage some of the theory of structuralism. The structuralist approach is, as I understand it, a search for the underlying pattern inherent in human phenomena. Fredric Jameson described it as "a double movement of analysis and synthesis," first to find the model and then demonstrate its validity. "The application of such a model," he says, "is thus complete only when, having disengaged the basic deep structure, the analyst is then able to generate back up out of it not only the original text but all the other variants of which the model is susceptible as well. It is this generational mechanism which the Structuralists call a *combinatoire*. Ideally, therefore, such analysis presupposes a body or corpus of texts."[7] These remarks are understood to apply rather widely: to a body of versions of myth, to grammar, to dreams perhaps—the wide range of phenomena in which structuralists busy themselves. I propose that the translations of these HB poems offer us a very rich study and a testing ground for some structuralist notions, just because we have in the Hebrew poem a strong and demonstrable structure—unknown to many, indeed, but once known, quite incontrovertibly *there;* and then for that desirable "body or corpus of texts," what more gloriously broad and rich range of them could one ever hope to find? I propose to look at some translations of one Hebrew poem, discover its "structure," and consider whether it constitutes a "generational mechanism." My argument is that what is common to all versions must be what exists in the original. It would be odd indeed, if a myriad of translators happened to hit on a similar shape. I propose a sort of game, then, that we hypothesize an *Ursprache,* an *Urpsalm* from which all these translations sprang, and this *Urpsalm,* if we are right, will coincide with the Hebrew structure.

We have resources: some biblical scholars are engaged in sophisticated but accessible form analyses in which the Hebrew is transliterated and commented on. One of the most distinguished of these scholars is David Noel Freedman, who reveals, in various passages and whole poems, symmetries and patterns of great beauty. For instance, in his "Structure of Psalm 137" (the great one beginning "By the waters of Babylon"), after a careful demonstration he concludes:

Psalm 137 is characterized by an envelope construction in which the outer sections fold around the inner ones producing a cohesive and integrated whole. Thus the opening and closing sections (vss. 1–2 and 8–9) form an *inclusio* which is keyed on the word Bābel. The body of the poem, likewise, consists of an outer shell, vss. 3 and 7, and an inner core, vss. 4–6. Even this core follows the same pattern, with vss. 4 and 6 cd forming a frame around the nucleus at the very center of the poem. This nucleus is an artfully designed chiastic couplet ["If I forget thee, O Jerusalem, may my right arm wither; / may my tongue stick to my palate, if I remember thee not!"] which is at once the dramatic high point or apex of the poem, and the axis linking the parts and exhibiting the essential structure of the whole (vss. 5–6 ab).[8]

Freedman supports his delineation of this structure with evidence of corroborative sound patterns, such as syllable count, alliteration, and onomatopoeia; he draws on the rich recent studies of analogues and origins in Canaanite, Akkadian, and Egyptian poetry and on the folkloric studies such as Theodore H. Gaster's. In the particular case of Psalm 137, the central pivotal double chiasm becomes in the King James Version only a single chiasm; but I think it can be said—and this is the remarkable thing—that all Freedman's other observations on structure are valid for the King James Version and for the other translations. The form has been translated. In another analysis, of the great "Storm" Psalm (29), Freedman observes that "a structural analysis of the psalm not only supports the integrity of the present text but also points to some complex and sophisticated techniques of Hebrew poetry."[9] Professor Stanley Gevirtz, in another study of some of the most ancient poems of the HB (The Women's Eulogy of Saul and David, Lamech's Song, Isaac's Blessing over Jacob, Balaam's first "Mashal," and David's Lament for Saul and Jonathan), insists again on the sophisticated literary craftsmanship of the Hebrew poets. And he warns: "To be indifferent toward their art is to risk indifference for their meaning."[10] I hope even the little samples I have already shown do demonstrate the special interdependence of form and meaning in these poems. One may hear them vaguely, enjoying the good rhythms and beautiful decorum of the KJV, or of Jerome, but one cannot really appropriate them without some awareness of the parallel patterns.

The fact is, although the forms are perfectly well known to biblical scholars, these texts are not even thought of as poems by many literate people, or even literary people. Robert Lowell was one of the few who knew that these poems persist even "when their translators merely intended prose and were forced by the structure of their originals to write poetry."[11] Marianne Moore was more like the rest of us: speaking of Habakkuk, she observes loosely, "Hebrew Poetry is prose with a sort of heightened consciousness" ("The Past Is the Present"). We need not be so intuitional. We have, I suggest, evidence that it is the translatable poetic form that "heightens the consciousness." In this case of Marianne Moore, it is ironic to note that Habakkuk contains some of the most elegantly patterned of psalms.[12]

To review, then.[13] Fully one-third of the HB is poetic in form, particularly, of course, Psalms, Proverbs, Song of Songs, Job, and the Prophets; and certain poems occur in prose contexts in other books. Hebrew manuscripts occasionally show awareness of parallel structure, but generally not; and Greek, Latin, Syriac, and Aramaic texts give no evidence. "It is astonishing," writes Norman K. Gottwald, "that the formal structure of ancient Hebrew poetry was transmitted through the centuries generally intact in spite of the lack of poetic format, even though the older forms were no longer employed in contemporary poetry and were, in fact, largely disregarded in biblical exegesis." The landmark in modern scholarship is the work of Bishop Lowth of Oxford, who in 1753 presented the parallelism of members as the fundamental formal feature of Hebrew verse.[14] Gottwald is able with what is now known of Ugaritic (i.e., Canaanite), Egyptian, and Akkadian analogues to declare that this parallelism, "virtually a mode of thought" in Near Eastern literary culture, was brought to its fullest artistic consummation by the Hebrew poets. He explains, moreover, how knowledge of the form is necessary to exegesis and how the parallelism "sustains and prolongs" the effect. "Faithful study of even a limited number of parallelisms will vastly enhance that sixth sense by which the compression and amplification of poetic thought is grasped almost intuitively."

Let us now, as Gottwald suggests, spell out a pattern and observe its quality in various versions. And then I should like—with the help of some notions from the structuralists—to consider those aspects that Gottwald indicates by the words "sustains and prolongs," "sixth sense," "compression and amplification of poetic thought," "grasped," "intuitively." Perhaps structuralist theory may help us toward a greater degree of specificity and precision in considering those processes that Gottwald rightly but loosely indicates.

The example I take is Psalm 24, for one thing because it is short and therefore comparatively manageable, and for another, because it is famous, partly through Handel.[15] Furthermore, where many psalms are private and personal, this one seems quite obviously public and ceremonial and thereby suggests connections with patterns in cultural anthropology. But I want to say the choice is not closely considered; the psalm does not even show a particularly high degree of structure or pattern. In fact, perhaps the connections between parts are more obscure than in others, for we do not know the ritual. In the more private psalms we can recognize familiar psychological progressions.

Here is the KJV of the psalm as it is conventionally printed (the italicized words are, of course, the elements the translators wanted to indicate as inserted without counterpart in the Hebrew; the meaning and function of *selah* are still not known for sure):

1   The earth *is* the Lord's, and the fulness thereof; the world, and they that dwell therein.
2   For he hath founded it upon the seas, and established it upon the floods.
3   Who shall ascend into the hill of the Lord? or who shall stand in his holy place?
4   He that hath clean hands, and a pure heart; who hath not lifted up his soul unto vanity, nor sworn deceitfully.
5   He shall receive the blessing from the Lord, and righteousness from the God of his salvation.
6   This *is* the generation of them that seek him, that seek thy face, O Jacob. Selah.
7   Lift up your heads, O ye gates; and be ye lift up, ye everlasting doors; and the King of glory shall come in.
8   Who *is* this King of glory? The Lord strong and mighty, the Lord mighty in battle.
9   Lift up your heads, O ye gates; even lift *them* up, ye everlasting doors, and the King of glory shall come in.
10   Who is this King of glory? The Lord of hosts, he *is* the King of glory. Selah.

Now let me present the same version divided according to its parallel structure. I have numbered the units 1 through 28, and lettered them to indicate relationships, and there follows a commentary on the relationships.

King James Version:

```
1, 2  The earth is the Lord's     and the fulness thereof    ⎫ ab
3, 4  The world                   and they that dwell therein ⎬ ab
                                                              ⎭

  5  For he hath founded it upon the seas    ⎫ c
  6  and       established it upon the floods ⎬ c
                                             ⎭

  7     Who shall ascend into the hill of the Lord? ⎫ d        ⎤
  8  or who shall stand   in his holy place?        ⎬ d        ⎬ Q
                                                    ⎭          ⎦

  9          He that hath clean hands       ⎫ e        ⎤
 10          and        a pure heart        ⎬ e        ⎥
 11          who hath not lifted up his soul unto vanity ⎫ f   ⎬ A₁
 12                     nor sworn deceitfully            ⎬ f   ⎥
                                                         ⎭    ⎦

 13  He shall receive the blessing from the Lord    ⎫ g       ⎤
 14  and              righteousness from the God    ⎬ g       ⎥
                                    of his salvation ⎭         ⎥
                                                              ⎬ A₂
 15  This is the generation of them that seek him              ⎥
 16                             that seek thy face, ⎫ h        ⎥
                                    O Jacob          ⎬ h       ⎦
                                                    ⎭

 17  Lift up your heads,   O ye gates           ⎫ i
 18  and be ye lift up,    ye everlasting doors ⎬ i
 19          and the King of glory shall come in  j

 20  Who is this King of glory?               k       ⎤ Q
 21          The Lord strong and mighty  ⎫ l  ⎬
 22          The Lord mighty in battle   ⎬ l  ⎦ A
                                         ⎭

 23  Lift up your heads,    O ye gates          ⎫ i
 24  even lift them up,     ye everlasting doors ⎬ i
 25          and the King of glory shall come in   j

 26  Who is this King of glory?               k       ⎤ Q
27, 28  The Lord of hosts, he is the King of glory  l, k ⎬ A
                                                      ⎦
```

1, 2, 3, 4 are an *abab* quatrain, *earth* matching *world*, and *fulness* matching *they that dwell*. Extrasyntactical meaning is that there are many earth dwellers, a *fulness* of them; the earth is described in human terms, in terms of its dwellers; and thereby the degree of God's possession of men is the stronger.

5, 6 rhyme *cc*, in that creation takes place upon the *wet*, *founded* and *established* working together to give a strong sense of stablility informed on the unstable wet element.

abab rhyme with *cc*, two earth statements with two water statements.

7, 8 rhyme *dd*, in that both are questions asking who is worthy to go into the holy hill. *dd* relates to 1 through 6, in that the Lord being very great, one might well think not just anyone could go into his sanctuary.

9, 10 rhyme *ee*, matching physical metaphor with spiritual abstraction, the one explaining the other.

11, 12 rhyme *ff*, in that both are negatives and match abstract (*vanity*) with real (*deceit*).

9–12 *ee* rhymes with *ff*, in that both identify the worthy, one positively, the other negatively.

eeff are a quatrain answering the question of *dd*.

13, 14 rhyme *gg*, both describing the benefits to the worthy in terms of *receiving*.

15, 16 rhyme *hh*, both affirming the identity of the worthy.

13–16 *gghh* form a quatrain all mentioning the deity, *receiving from* balancing *seeking*. Identities now being established by question and answer, full and certain, the procession (which may have been for the entry of the Ark into the temple, or the New Year entry of the God into the temple in the Canaanite tradition) may now take place.

17, 18 rhyme *ii*, imperative apostrophes to the entryway, extravagant metaphor, one active, the other passive. Combination of active and passive seems to give more power.

19 *j* by itself for the moment.

20 is *k*, demands the credentials of the entity in *j*.

21, 22 rhyme *ll*, two overlapping epithets for the entity, both military.

23, 24 repeat *ii* above, what the French might call rime riche.

25, 19 rhyme *jj*, rime riche.

26, 20 rhyme *kk*, rime riche.

27, 28 sum up the question and answer definitively, 27 being *l* to rhyme with *ll* (the military figure), and 28 being *k*, repeating the epithet of *kk*.

Note also the repetition of the *jk* sequence (19–20 and 25–26), another set of rhymes.

The whole divides itself into three large units: 1 through 6 states the relationship of deity to mankind; 7 through 16 is man-centered, a kind of choice of the elect consequent on the relationship stated; 17 through 28 is deity-centered, a celebration by the elect. The man-centered section is parallel to the deity-centered section in that both are in antiphonal form. The progression of parts has a psychological validity, a "natural" sort of logic and ease without relational words; and the triumphant conclusion unfolds out of the humble certainty of the beginning, and refers back to it, making of the whole a sublimely decorous ceremony.

Here follow the eight other versions: two in English, the French Bible de Jérusalem, Luther, the Septuagint, Jerome, and then a Turkish one, to provide an example of a non-Indo-European language (Turkish is the only such language I have any competence in), and then finally the Urpsalm, the Hebrew.[15] I have tried to select versions that are, like the vulgate, not dependent on an intermediate text. They are printed to reveal the structure, and I believe my analysis of the KJV structure applies to all these versions. I would hope other scholars would compare other versions.

New English Bible	Book of Common Prayer

New English Bible

The earth is the Lord's   and all that is in it
The world   and they that dwell therein

For it was he who founded it upon the seas
              and planted it firm upon the waters
                                                    beneath

        Who may go up the mountain of the Lord?
and who may stand in his holy place?

    He who has clean hands
        and a pure heart
    who has not set his mind on falsehood
    and has not committed prejury

He shall receive a blessing from the Lord
              and justice from God his Saviour

Such is the fortune of those who seek him
              who seek the face of the
                              God of Jacob

Lift up your heads, you gates
Lift yourselves up, you everlasting doors
    that the King of glory may come in

Who is the King of glory?
        The Lord strong and mighty
        The Lord mighty in battle

Lift up your heads, you gates
Lift them up,   you everlasting doors
    that the King of glory may come in

Who then is the King of glory?

The King of glory is the Lord of hosts

Book of Common Prayer

The earth is the Lord's   and all that therein is
The compass of the world   and they that dwell therein

For he hath founded it upon the seas
and   prepared it upon the floods

        Who shall ascend into the hill of the Lord?
or who shall rise up in his holy place?

            Even he that hath clean hands
                and a pure heart

        and that hath not lift up his mind unto vanity
                    nor sworn to deceive his neighbour

He shall receive the blessing from the Lord
        and   righteousness from the God of his
                                              salvation

This is the generation of them that seek him
even   of them that seek thy face
                                          O Jacob

Lift up your heads,   O ye gates
and be ye lift up,   ye everlasting doors
    and the King of glory shall come in

Who is the King of glory?
    It is the Lord strong and mighty
    even the Lord mighty in battle

Lift up your heads,   O ye gates
and be ye lift up,   ye everlasting doors
    and the King of glory shall come in

Who is the King of glory?

Even the Lord of hosts, he is the King of glory

La Bible de Jérusalem	Luther's Version

La Bible de Jérusalem

À Yahvé la terre et sa plénitude
le monde et tout son peuplement

C'est lui qui   l'a fondée sur les mers
et sur les fleuves l'a fixée

Qui montera sur la montagne de Yahvé?
et qui se tiendra dans son lieu saint?

L'homme aux mains nettes
au   coeur pur
Son âme ne se porte pas vers des riens
il ne jura pas pour tromper.

Il emportera la bénédiction de Yahvé
et   la justice du Dieu de son salut

C'est la race de ceux qui Le cherchent
qui recherchent sa face, Dieu de Jacob

Portes, levez vos frontons
elevez-vous, portails antiques
qu'il entre, le roi de gloire

Qui est-il, ce roi de gloire?
C'est Yahvé, le fort, le vaillant
Yahvé le vaillant des combats

Portes, levez vos frontons
elevez-vous, portails antiques
qu'il entre, le roi de gloire

Qui est-il, ce roi de gloire?

Yahvé Sabaot, c'est lui, le roi de gloire

Luther's Version

Die Erde ist des Herrn, und was darinnen ist
der Erdboden   und was darauf wohnet

Denn Er hat ihn an die Meere gegründet
an den Wassern bereitet

Wer wird auf des Herrn Berg gehen?
und wer wird stehen an seiner heiligen Stätte?

Der unschuldige Hände hat
und reinen Herzens ist

Der nicht Lust hat zu loser Lehre
und schwöret nicht fälschlich

Der wird den Segen vom Herrn empfangen
und   Gerechtigkeit von dem Gott seines Heils

Da ist das Geschlecht, das nach ihm fraget
und das da suchet dein Antlitz,
Jakob

Machet die Thore weit
und die Thüren in der Welt hoch
dass der König der Ehren einziehe

Wer ist derselbe König der Ehren?
Es ist der Herr stark und mächtig
der Herr mächtig im Streit

Machet die Thore weit
und die Thüren in der Welt hoch
dass der König der Ehren einziehe

Wer ist derselbe König der Ehren?

Es ist der Herr Zabaoth, Er ist der König der Ehren

Jerome's Version	Kitabı Mukaddes (Istanbul, 1972)

Jerome's Version

Domini est terra, et plenitudo ejus
　　　orbis terrarum, et universi, qui habitant
　　　　　　　in eo

Quia ipse super maria fundavit eum:
　　　et super flumina praeparavit eum

　　Quis ascendet in montem Domini?
aut quis stabit in loco sancto ejus?

　　Innocens manibus
　　　et mundo corde
　　Qui non accepit in vano animam suam
　　　nec juravit in dolo proximo suo

Hic accipiet benedictionem a Domino
et　　　　　　misericordiam a Deo salutari suo

Haec est generatio quaerentium eum
　　　　　quaerentium faciem Dei Jacob

Attollite portas principes vestras
et elevamini, portae aeternales
　　et introibit rex gloriae
Quis est iste rex gloriae?
　　Dominus fortis et potens
　　Dominus potens in proelio

Attollite portas principes vestras
et elevamini, portae aeternales
　　et introibit rex gloriae

Quis est iste rex gloriae?
Dominus virtutum ipse est rex gloriae

Kıtabı Mukaddes (Istanbul, 1972)

Rabbindir yeryüzü	ve onun doluluğu
Dünya	ve onda oturanlar

Çünkü onu denizler üzerine kurdu
　Ve ırmaklar uzerinde onu durdurdu

Rabbin dağına　　　kim çıkacak?
Ve mukaddes makamında kim duracak?

O adam ki,　　elleri temizdir
　　　　ve yüreği paktır
　Gönlünü yalana vermemiştir
　Hile ile de yemin etmemiştir

O Rabden bereket
Ve kurtuluşunun Allahından salâh alacaktır

Bu onu arıyanların
Senin yüzünü araş　anların neslidir, Yakubdur

Ey kapılar, başlarınızı yükseltin
Ve yükselin, ey ebedî kapılar
　Ve izzet Kıralı girecek

Kimdir o izzet Kıralı?
　Kudretli ve cebbar olan Rab
　Cenkte cebbar olan Rabdir

Ey kapılar, baslarınızı yükseltin
Ve yükselin, ey ebedî kapılar
　Ve izzet Kıralı girecek

Kimdir o izzet Kıralı?

Ordularin Rabbi; İzzet Kıralı odur

Τοῦ Κυρίου ἡ γη καὶ τὸ πλήρωμα αὐτῆς
  ἡ οἰκουμένη καὶ πάντες οἱ κατοικοῦντες
        ἐν αὐτῇ

Αὐτὸς ἐπὶ θαλασσῶν ἐθεμελίωσεν αὐτὴν
  καὶ ἐπὶ ποταμῶν ἡτοίμασεν αὐτήν

  Τίς ἀναβήσεται εἰς τὸ ὄρος τοῦ Κυρίου
καὶ τίς στήσεται ἐν τόπῳ ἁγίωι αὐτοῦ;
  Ἀθῷος χερσὶν
καὶ καθαρὸς τῇ καρδίᾳ
    ὃς οὐκ ἔλαβεν ἐπὶ ματαίῳ τὴν ψυχὴν αὐτοῦ
    καὶ οὐκ ὤμοσεν ἐπὶ δόλῳ τῷ πλησίον αὐτοῦ

Οὗτος λήμψεται εὐλογίαν παρὰ Κυρίου
  καὶ ἐλεημοσύνην   παρὰ θεοῦ σωτῆρος αὐτοῦ

    Αὕτη ἡ γενεὰ ζητούντων αὐτὸν
      ζητούντων τὸ πρόσωπον τοῦ θεοῦ
              Ἰακωβ

Ἄρατε πύλας οἱ ἄρχοντες ὑμῶν
καὶ ἐπάρθητε πύλαι αἰώνιοι
    καὶ εἰσελεύσεται ὁ βασιλεὺς τῆς δόξης

  Τίς ἐστιν οὗτος ὁ βασιλεὺς τῆς δόξης;
    Κύριος κραταιὸς καὶ δυνατός
    Κύριος δυνατὸς ἐν πολέμῳ

Ἄρατε πύλας οἱ ἀρχοντες ὑμῶν
καὶ ἐπάρθητε πύλαι αἰώνιοι
    καὶ εἰσελεύσεται ὁ βασιλεὺς τῆς δόξης

Τίς ἐστιν οὗτος ὁ βασιλεὺς τῆς δόξης; ·
Κύριος τῶν δυνάμεων, αὐτός ἐστιν οὗτος
        ὁ βασιλεὺς τῆς δόξης

לַיהוָה הָאָרֶץ וּמְלוֹאָהּ
תֵּבֵל וְיֹשְׁבֵי בָהּ
כִּי־הוּא עַל־יַמִּים יְסָדָהּ
וְעַל נְהָרוֹת יְכוֹנְנֶהָ
מִי־יַעֲלֶה בְּהַר־יְהוָה
וּמִי־יָקוּם בִּמְקוֹם קָדְשׁוֹ
נְקִי כַפַּיִם
וּבַר־לֵבָב
אֲשֶׁר לֹא־נָשָׂא לַשָּׁוְא נַפְשִׁי
וְלֹא נִשְׁבַּע לְמִרְמָה
יִשָּׂא בְרָכָה מֵאֵת יְהוָה
וּצְדָקָה מֵאֱלֹהֵי יִשְׁעוֹ
זֶה דּוֹר דֹּרְשׁוֹ
מְבַקְשֵׁי פָנֶיךָ יַעֲקֹב
שְׂאוּ שְׁעָרִים רָאשֵׁיכֶם
וְהִנָּשְׂאוּ פִּתְחֵי עוֹלָם
וְיָבוֹא מֶלֶךְ הַכָּבוֹד
מִי זֶה מֶלֶךְ הַכָּבוֹד
יְהוָה עִזּוּז וְגִבּוֹר
יְהוָה גִּבּוֹר מִלְחָמָה ·
שְׂאוּ שְׁעָרִים רָאשֵׁיכֶם
וּשְׂאוּ פִּתְחֵי עוֹלָם
וְיָבֹא מֶלֶךְ הַכָּבוֹד
מִי הוּא זֶה מֶלֶךְ הַכָּבוֹד
יְהוָה צְבָאוֹת   הוּא מֶלֶךְ הַכָּבוֹד

The spectrum of language here is, of course, limited. For a phenomenally wide experience of world languages and Bible translation, we may turn to Eugene Nida and his work, based in the Christian missionary movement.[16] It is the missionaries' conviction that the Bible can be made available, and it is their vocation to make it so. They naturally weigh the CB most, and very little of it is in verse. However, I cannot imagine—and this may be a defect in my imagination—any translation of the poetry that does not preserve the parallelisms. If any language structure is innate, or fits the constitution of the brain, Chomsky-wise, surely it is this. To be human is to be able to paraphrase. This is Steiner's point: to understand a thing is to translate it. In the Hebrew parallelisms called synonymous, the a_2 of the couplet is a "translation" of the a_1, although in the same language. And just as the relationship carries over into Latin or English, I think it must carry over into Choctaw or Japanese as well. And the meaning has the better chance of surviving because the translator makes two approximations of it. The margin of error is reduced. This parallelism is, I propose, a great protector of meaning, whatever the language of translation. The peculiar structure of Hebrew verse, then, combined with pious care in copying and translating, is a great self-preserving mechanism.

It is true that there are some qualities of the Hebrew language other than poetic structure that tend to work for a high degree of congruence in translations. One is a strong tendency toward the concrete. The formulation of the Law is the extent, perhaps, of the Hebrew abstractive genius; Hebrew "Wisdom," as in other Near Eastern wisdom literatures, consists of discrete proverbs, in series. Israel was a poet, as Arnold says. And so he anthropomorphized, and reified, and dealt in figures. Not for him the force-not-ourselves-that-makes-for-righteousness, or the stream-of-tendency-by-which-all-things-seek-to-fulfill-the-law-of-their-being,[17] but a burning bush, the voice from the whirlwind, a father, a shepherd, a pillar of fire, a fortress, a refiner's fire, the wielder of the plumb line, the winnower, the treader of the grapes. Nida proposes that the Bible is accessible in translation because the culture it is based in is the most widespread type, both temporally and like other cultures geographically. I suppose one might agree: the various cultural phases—nomadic herdsman, slave, subsistence farmer—these are basic and widespread modes of life. But I think the point is that the Hebrew used these basics as metaphors for abstract things, and it is that which helps to keep the texts translatable and accessible. That—along with the device of self-glossing that the parallelism affords. Our exemplary psalm gives us "He that hath clean hands and a pure heart"; the difficult abstraction of *pure heart* is unequivocally explained by the very accessible metaphor of *clean hands*. In ritual, literal handwashing efficiently symbolizes spiritual cleansing. Psalm 103 explains "who forgiveth all thy iniquities" with its rhyming parallel "who healeth all thy diseases"; again, the spiritual statement is unequivocally explained by the physical. Indeed, the prophet Hosea himself seems to make a literary comment with his own quatrain:

I have also spoken by the prophets	*a*
have multiplied visions	*b*
used similitudes	*b*
by the ministry of the prophets.	*a*

(Hos. 12:10)

This appears to be poetry about its own poetic method: to *use similitudes* is precisely what these pairs of abstract-concrete rhymes do; and by *multiplying visions,* or giving us sets of visual images, they explain each other and protect meanings. The multiplying is the parallelism: A × 2, or A × 3.

The economy and brilliance of HB metaphor remain one of the literary wonders of the world. Hebrew does not, on the other hand, rely much on adjectives and adverbs—it is poor in modifiers and verb variants—and these paucities make for a simple sentence structure. It is, moreover, poor in relational words, as compared with, say, Greek. It is to the Greeks we owe that supple logic that can lead us through complicated linear processes of reasoning, of which I take Euclidian chain of thought to be the very type. Such Greek is heavily hypotactic, that is, very explicit on relationships making much use of subordination, while Hebrew is paratactic, depending on juxtaposition of elements, or coordination. (Greek poetry—Homer, for instance—can be highly paratactic.) Though the effect of parataxis can be said to be more engaging emotionally, or more "poetic," one can hardly say it is less intellectual. For the reader or hearer actively correlates the two members, the pair of "rhyming" ideas, by discovering the logic of similarity or contrast. In Isa. 55:13:

Instead of the thorn	*a*
shall come up the firtree	*b*
Instead of the brier	*a*
shall come up the myrtle tree	*b*
And it shall be to the Lord for a name	*c*
For an everlasting sign that shall not be cut off	*c*

the promise of relief cannot be grasped without intellection; one must relate *c* to *c* to get the message that the *name* (or enduring renown) of the Lord is *what is everlasting*. This is consonant in fact with the famous *I am that I am*, or *I am what endures*, and helps us translate the peculiar progressive of the Hebrew verb, which is neither past, present, nor future. It is really astonishing that the orthodox exegetes have pondered the parallel structure so little. To neglect the art is to neglect the meaning (Gevirtz, quoted previously). Furthermore, as the Hebrew scholar Samuel Sandmel says, the parallelism provides the shades of meaning, making good the lack of modifiers, the paucity of verbs, and the inability to form compound words.[18] One feels no lack; the idiom is dense, pregnant, and perhaps easier to apprehend than Euclidian reasoning. "For the Jews require a sign, and the Greeks seek after wisdom," said Paul (1 Cor. 1:22). This may be taken as a comment on the difference in linguistic modes.

To sum up: these differences between Greek and Hebrew, which of course have been much explored and commented on, reveal the Hebrew as comparatively translatable—its short statements, its preponderance of simple nouns and verbs, its concreteness, its parataxis—all these things transfer comparatively easily into another language. How *easy* Jerome's Latin is, compared, for example, to Caesar's. And Luther had little need to resort to those difficult compounds that his language uses for abstractions. The peculiar excellence of the KJV as compared to other English versions is not the subject of this essay, but we should note here that those great translators for the most part kept the earlier simpler English rather than the involved, more hypotactic baroque that was developing in their own time.

These qualities of Hebrew vocabulary and syntax apply to all of the HB, not only to the conspicuous formality of poetry, and certainly Hebrew seems to suffer no incapacity in history or narrative. Since I want to consider the elements of form in poetry, however, I want to note here the elements of form in its largest sense, in the whole. The great literary fictions of epic and drama and romance, what we call plots, are said to impose shape, stability, and meaning on the flux of experience. And if the deity is the "supreme fiction," why then the "supreme plot" is that of the Bible—the whole thing, from Creation through to Apocalypse. And while the Greeks seem to have had a cyclical sense of history, and their practice in history is sectional—as with Thucydides and Herodotus—and while we in the twentieth century have a sense of history as fragmentary and relative, the Hebrews had a ruling idea of history as revelatory of divine purpose, their ruling motive in the recording of it a pious one that informs the whole. And so it has a religious oneness that can also be taken as an artistic unity, with a strong relationship of parts to whole.

> This *is* the purpose that is purposed
> > upon the whole earth: *a*
> And this *is* the hand that is stretched
> > out upon all the nations.   *a*
> For the Lord of hosts hath purposed,
> > and who shall disannul *it*?   *b*
> And his hand *is* stretched out,
> > and who shall turn it back?   *b*
>
> > > > > > > > > > (Isa. 14:26–27)

Perhaps this sense of form in the largest things transfers itself to a sense of form in small poems. Certainly there was a pious impulse in these biblical writings; at any rate, the form of parallel structures that was common among the surrounding cultures, a "mode of thought," developed in the hands of these Hebrew poets possessed by a passionate sense of the sacredness of verbal record into a consummate art form.

It is common these days to speak of form as "spatial," for we feel that something happens in art forms that changes ordinary linear time. Something is created that takes us out of time, and the flux of experience is somehow stabilized. In life, we are indeed conscious of more than the instant that is reality; we create, says Bergson, *durées*, or minimal plots. We make or borrow some larger plot, too; we have a worldview.[19] We look before and after. In narrative art, we are still more conscious of plot than we are in life: we remember and use "clues," we relate discrepancies by irony, we anticipate endings. And in poetry, we generally look before and after more than we do in prose; for poetry is generally more highly patterned. By patterns, the poem makes many references back upon itself and sets up many anticipations, and its resolutions often function in many dimensions. And so it seems that something solid and objective is precipitated out of the flux. Hence those many statements by the poets themselves that they have defeated time: Horace says of his poems, *Exegi monumentum aere perennius*, "I have built a monument more lasting than bronze," and consequently, *non omnis moriar*, "I shall not altogether die" (*Carminum Liber* 3, 30); and Shakespeare follows suit, "Not marble nor the gilded monuments of princes / Shall outlive this powerful rhyme," and "Death to me subscribes" (*Sonnets* 53, 107).

What, then, of the formal element common to all these translations of Psalm 24? The sound patterns, obviously, are not transferable, language to language, except when there are actual repetitions within the poem itself—refrains, that is, and, of course, proper nouns. And yet the essential pattern prevails, the parallelisms that are the radical formal element of Hebrew verse. By these patterns, the poem refers back to itself, sets up expectations within itself, and resolves itself. Those who are familiar with traditional musical form will recognize a strong similarity: repetitions with variations, paired phrases, refrains, da capos, resolutions, and tonality. But the remarkable thing is that although the form is "musical," the patterns are not of sound but of meaning. The sense unit coincides with the form unit, constitutes, in fact, the form unit. It is what Ernest Renan called a *rime des pensées*,[20] a rhyme of thoughts, or a music of ideas. It all lends itself to music supremely well—witness a thousand psalm settings now in scores of Western music—and it is hard to imagine that it did not originally move to music, most probably dance as well. Psalm 24 is sometimes thought to be the very song to which David danced in that memorable procession before the Ark. The psalm form we can muse on *diachronically*, as Saussure would say, by considering its historical origin, its place in the Hebrew cultus, its liturgical or artistic adaptation in European culture. But it may also be considered *synchronically*, the thing in itself. Philip E. Lewis quotes Merleau-Ponty: "Esthetic expression confers upon what it expresses existence in itself (*en soi*), implants it in nature as something perceived and accessible to everyone," and notes that it is music that is the supreme example of such expression; with the sonata of Vinteuil, Proust "realizes that the musical sounds are not signs of musical meaning but the very substance of the sonata descending within us."[21] This biblical verse seems to me the kind in which content and form are most closely tied together, of all examples of literary art the one that approaches most closely to the condition of music, where the form is the thing itself. I would suggest that this is so, just because the units are units of verbal sense. One is not fitting one mode to another, not fitting words *to* music, content *to* form. Subject, meaning, and form all seem to become a continuum.

Elements of the interdisciplinary structuralist approach remain illuminating for these poems in their translatable essence. For the structure is defined as an "instrument of coherence"[22] often discovered as in mathematics by reduction into isomorphisms that suggest the paired Hebrew *stichoi;* the structure is said to be reversible as in mathematics, and as in the frequent "ring structure" and frequent chiasmus in Hebrew verse. The chiasmus can be not only *a b b a* but at times *a b c c b a,* as here:

Make the *heart* of this people fat	*a*
and make their *ears* heavy	*b*
and shut their *eyes;*	*c*
lest they see with their *eyes*	*c*
and hear with their *ears,*	*b*
And understand with their *heart.* . . .	*a*

(Isa. 6:10; my italics)

"A structure," it is said, "is a system of transformations . . . which consumes itself or enriches itself by the very play of its transformations."[23] This is understood to apply to grammars, mathematics, psychology, and anthropology, but it seems to me that our Hebrew poem is the most positively exemplary of all in its "play of transformations."

Let us take the principle of self-conservation. Given the nature of the Hebrew language in general, and how it has a relatively high degree of translatableness to start with, the formal parallelisms of its verse make it so much more emphatically self-conserving. To compare the prose, we may turn to Jean Starobinski's admirable analysis of the story of the Gadarene swine (Mark 5:1–20).[24] Here, it is true, we do not have the original; but there is no reason to think our Greek *koine* does not represent the Aramaic pretty closely. The simple syntactic structures and the metaphors are the sorts of things the *koine* can reproduce. And, as Starobinski says, since it is canonical we have reason to believe the writers strove for the utmost exactitude, for pious reasons. This is the evangel itself. Even so, however, as it goes through the long process of transformations, or translations, there are a myriad of points at which the translator must make a lexical choice. Vocabularies of two different languages never offer equivalents. And since this text is so very important for doctrine and since the translator's purpose is pious, not "literary," *every* choice is governed by an element of dogma. And in succeeding levels of translation, the text becomes more and more deeply imbued with dogma. Starobinski opens his analysis with a challenge: Can you read an evangelical text in a "purely literary" way? Hardly. The religious purpose is of the essence. Although it is piety that motivates the preservation of the text, this same piety progressively "skews" (the word is Nida's) the sense in translations, and modifies the meaning, if not indeed shaping it.[25]

Starobinski certainly sees the narrative of the Gadarene swine as a structure, but he grants that the self-conservation of the text is limited by doctrinal assumptions and kerygmatic purpose. I propose that Hebrew poetry by virtue of its form is more self-conserving than prose, whether evangelical or historical. Because the poem is more of a whole, the consistency of parts is more self-protective. Hebrew a_1 is to Hebrew a_2 as Latin a_1 is to Latin a_2, as Luther's a_1 is to Luther's a_2. Furthermore, Hebrew *a b b a* is to Hebrew *c d d c* as Latin *a b b a* is to Latin *c d d c*, as Luther's *a b b a* is to Luther's *c d d c*. To a degree, the texts are self-exegetical (the pure heart *explains* the clean hands); insofar as a_2 parallels a_1, the spectrum of translators' choices becomes radically limited. Because the one element answers to the other in some way, the meaning is more likely to survive. And all this is due to that important fact that in the Hebrew the sense unit is the form unit. The units are not phonemic but semantic.

Yet, although the structure basis is not of sounds, the structure itself is analogous to musical structures in its isomorphisms, refrains, themes and variations, tonality, totality. And the claim that Hebrew verse is particularly exemplary of structuralist theory connects, then, with Lévi-Strauss's insight that music offers the very type of structural activity, as he outlines it in the pages concluding his "Overture" to *Le Cru et le cuit:* "The structure of myths is revealed through means of a score." He enumerates elements common to myth and music that, to my mind, apply even more to this—may one say—tangibly self-conserving poem structure. With both myth and music,

> Each requires at every instance a temporal dimension in order to become manifest. . . . Both, in effect, are mechanisms designed to do away with time. Underneath the sounds and rhythms, music operates on a rough terrain which is the physiological time of the listener; that time is irremediably diachronic because it is irreversible; music none the less transmutes the segment of that time which is devoted to listening into a totality which is synchronic and enclosed in itself. The act of listening to the musical work has immobilized the passage of time because of the work's internal organization. . . . In listening to music— and while we are listening—we have achieved a kind of immortality.[26]

This is extreme, but Lévi-Strauss brings us back, in what is surely a very sound way, to the physiology to which we must return.[27] With music and with myth, he writes—and let us add poetry—there is "a double continuum." One is external: in music, the sounds; in myth, the events and narrative; in poetry, let us add, the syntactic or verbal units. The other is internal:

> It has its seat in the psycho-physiological time of the listener. . . . the periodicity of the cerebral waves and the organic rhythms, the capacity of memory, and the power of attention. These are neuro-psychical aspects which mythology especially challenges by the length of narration, by the recurrence of the themes, and by the other forms of recurrence and parallelism. In order to be properly taken in, mythology [or the poem] demands that the mind of the listener sweep thoroughly back and forth across the field of the narrative [or the poem] as it spreads out before him. . . . Aside from psychological time, music addresses itself to physiological and even visceral time. . . . All

counterpoint contains a mute part to be filled in by the cardiac and respiratory systems.[28]

Here is a piece of theory intended to apply to myth. I find it transformable and generative, an instrument of coherence that may help to discover the phenomenology of the Hebrew poem, or at least to define the area of our ignorance of that phenomenology. English-reading theorists will remember how Pater was reaching toward this same transformationalist idea when he declared, "All art approaches the condition of music."[29]

If there is something substantial in the school of psychology that claims the left side of the brain takes as its business mathematics, logic, and verbal activity, while the right side takes spatial and musical, then we might speculate that the combination of words with music calls forth a broadly integrated response.[30] I propose that the poetry of the HB, moreover, because it is a music of verbal concepts, makes this consummation in an especially broad way. Coleridge may be intimating this when he says that "the words of the Bible find me at greater depths of my being [than] all other books put together."[31] All this, however, can be no more than promising speculation. We are agreed, and have been for years, on the great beauty of these translated poems.

They have been neglected by literary scholars, and yet their influence and importance are incalculably great. Secular culture loses when it leaves these great texts to the theologians. By means of their metaphors and structures they extend our consciousness. While in Eastern culture there is the persistent idea that the most important things are unsayable, in Western culture I believe there is more of a sense of unlimited possibilities of poetry, just because these translated Hebrew poems have achieved the "impossible" so often. Our great poets of the seventeenth century, steeped in this verse, acknowledged its power more than we do. It is not to curry favor with the Author that Donne, for example, makes the following statement:

There are not so eloquent books in the world, as the Scriptures: Accept those names of Tropes and Figures, which the Grammarians and Rhetoricians have put upon us, and we may be bold to say, that in all their Authors, Greek and Latin, we cannot finde

so high, and so lively examples, as those Tropes, and those figures, as we may in the Scriptures: whatsoever hath justly delighted any man in any man's writing, is exceeded in the Scriptures.[32]

When Donne speaks so, he appears to be assuming that translation
is no impediment to this eloquence.

I want to insist on the validity of Bible translation as a most
remarkable literary phenomenon, and I hope I have suggested how
structuralist theory might help us to understand this phenomenon.
One further principle demands consideration. The element of totality
in a structure, says the structuralist, does not preclude the unit's
constituting a substructure of a larger structure, hierarchically.
Again, we have a mathematical analogue, in Gödelian limitations and
Gödelian hierarchy. One may even see the exigencies of the semantic
rhymes suggesting and finally developing, out of history and geography, the larger isomorphisms: Sodom rhymes with Gomorrah, Israel
rhymes with Judah, Tyre with Sidon, Gath with Eskalon, Dan with
Beersheba; the captivity in Egypt rhymes with the captivity in Babylon, the crossing of the Red Sea with the crossing of the Jordan, and
so on. These rhymes set precedents for Christian exegesis: old Adam
with the New, Old Testament with the New, Moses with Christ, Eve
with Mary, and now, in the example most interesting to linguists, the
Tower of Babel with Pentecost.[33] To suggest the hierarchy, let us start
with one line of verse rhyming with another; the couplet relates to
the strophe, the strophe to the psalm, the psalm to a section of the
psalter, made in five books, it is thought, to match the Pentateuch;
both pentateuchs being substructures of the HB—and then, in Christian terms, the Old Testament combining with the New, presumably
to constitute the Logos, the structure of structures.

The Hebrew structures, one may propose, have so far proved the
most transformational and the most generative of all, perhaps the
most used of all art forms, the most self-conserving, functioning as
musical constructs function; and yet the verbal translatable code is
more secure than music can ever be in scores or in performance
tradition. The actual Hebrew music of the poetry is lost; the medieval
music must be reconstructed with at least an element of hypothesis;
the Renaissance music is, a great deal of it, still current, reinforcing
and helping to keep current these great texts. But the verbal music,

renewed and preserved in translations, is structurally the same, and durable. The substance of music is the indistinguishable overlap of form and content, and this poetry partakes of that wholeness and is the more high powered because the music is of meanings.

Finally, to hypothesize the matrix structure: it *is* the Hebrew in a sense; but more properly it is what underlies the Hebrew as well as all the translations, and it can be represented with a diagram. Or one might try to make a model with the sort of materials physicists use for model atoms: color-coded plastic blocks for *stichoi*, with connecting wires to suggest lines of force, or orbits even. But meantime one might try some figures of speech rather than of plastic: the psalm structure is like a coiled spring, full of élan, energy that has renewed itself progressively, so far seeming inexhaustible. It is a "high-energy construct," a dynamo, a generator. It *demands* new music, new translations. "Sing a new song unto the Lord." To reveal and chart these generative models is to discover art in a new way; to contemplate their function may be to open new avenues in literary theory. They may cast light in unexpected ways. It is a question, for instance, how much the writers of the CB were conscious of Hebrew parallelistic structure as they studied the scriptures. Often the gospel writers seem ignorant of it, but Jesus himself was hardly so. When they asked him which was the great commandment, he gave them two:

> Thou shalt love the Lord thy God with all thy heart, and with all thy soul and with all thy mind. This is the first and great commandment. And the second is like unto it: Thou shalt love thy neighbor as thyself. On these two commandments hang all the law and the prophets. (Matt. 22:36–40)

It may be that in a flashing insight he saw the two as the same thing, as mutually explicatory parallels, one "like unto" the other.

Chapter 3

The Multiplication of Similitudes: An Essay on Teaching

Students in Bible-as-literature classes often bring an assortment of strained attitudes, ranging from that of the "believer" who may be fearful or suspicious to that of the atheist who comes in as a reductionist or scoffer.[1] One may at first ask the whole gamut of them to try to put aside the question Is it true? and look together at what is there. One might refer to Chesterton's idea—and there may be a little shock in this for some—that our myths and legends are the truest thing we have anyway. But from the first, as one accompanies students through selected readings of the historical books, one may invite attention to metaphor. What could be more innocent or more natural for the literature teacher to do? And yet I believe it gently leads into a kind of defusing of the charged attitudes of the students and ultimately to an intellectual enlargement and to a reading of the Bible that is richer and more rewarding—literarily, artistically, and, if one may say so, spiritually.

At the outset, it needs to be emphasized that there are two accounts of creation, the six-day account (Gen. 1–2:3) and the Adam and Eve account (Gen. 2:4–3:24). One may ask as a reading assignment that the students be ready to make some observations on the difference in kind between the two accounts. (The term *account* neatly sidesteps the issue of literal truth, where *story* or *myth* might raise hackles.) Students' observations can be gathered into a consensus that the first is comparatively abstract, austere, cosmological, while the second is concrete, homey, full of specificities: the names of Adam and Eve and the geography of Eden, ribs, fig leaves, a serpent, trees, and an anthropomorphic God who walks in the garden in the

45

cool of the day. One can sidestep the difficult doctrinal questions both accounts raise; in fact one must, or be forever embroiled to the neglect of literature and literary criticism. But one can insist on the two different styles and observe that the Adam and Eve account is composed earlier, and in an imagistic mode that is easier to visualize and grasp, in a mode called "primitive" or "naive"; while the six-day creation is on a higher level of abstraction, more philosophical and less imagistic, though the images are bold and magnificent. Borrowing from Kenneth Burke,[2] one might ask, How would you best present the idea that man is doomed to death, to toiling for bread, and woman to pain in childbirth? Answer: by a narrative such as that in Genesis 2–3. And how would you best present the principle of sublime order and essential good in creation? By a narrative such as Genesis 1.

The murder of Abel supplies us with a stunning isolated analyzable figure: "the voice of thy brother's blood crieth unto me from the ground" (Gen. 4:10). The matter of metaphor can get so enormously subtle that I think it is as well to be utterly simple, even simplistic, at first when one can be. Is this ordinary speech? What is remarkable about it? It is something *not true*. Is it a valid way to speak? Is it effective? Yes. It is very effective, very strong. Can it be said without the metaphor? Well, you would have to say, the earth, creation, seems to be outraged by this act; murder cannot stay hid but makes itself known to God; and so forth and so on. And it turns out that the metaphor is not only a powerful and engaging way of saying this but also very condensed. Students will consider the differentiation of metaphor and simile, but the distinction is not particularly useful here, and "metaphor" is best used in its largest sense, to cover all figurative language. It must be emphasized that metaphor is not a kind of "poetic" beautification or decoration but a mode of thinking indispensable even in science and philosophy, as is being increasingly acknowledged these days.[3]

The development of symbols can be suggested in the Noah material: the dove, the olive branch, the rainbow. One classifies most of Genesis as etiological material, explaining "beginnings" through metaphor and symbol. The account of the Tower of Babel, for instance, can be so emphasized—a way of thinking about our terrible misunderstandings of one another all over the earth and our consequent loss of power.

As part of a general program of raising metaphor consciousness, one mentions in passing how Jacob complains that Simeon and Levi in the Dinah incident have made his name to "stink" among the local people (Gen. 34:30); how the Midianites feared the presence of the children of Israel, that they should "lick up" the country, "as the ox licketh up the grass of the field" (Num. 22:4); how Moses in bitter black humor complains to God that he has to act as if he were a lactating father to his unruly group: "Have I conceived all this people? have I begotten them, that thou shouldst say unto me, Carry them in thy bosom, as a nursing father beareth the sucking child?" (Num. 11:12). Incidental to the historical account there occurs such a passage as God's reminder to the people in the wilderness of how he brought them up out of Egypt: "I bare you on eagle's wings" (Exod. 19:4) (what condensed nobility, strength, and *soaring*!). And then there are the metaphors in actual poems, such as David's comparison of Saul and Jonathan to "weapons of war" in the beautiful lament (2 Sam. 1:27).

At some time in dealing with the historical books it is well to raise the conventional old medieval idea of the fourfold exegesis, of, for the best example, the historical sequence of the escape from Egypt, the wandering in the wilderness, and the conquest of Canaan. First, the historical or literal interpretation: the Israelites did indeed escape from the real historical Egypt under Moses' leadership and did have many trials in the wilderness and did ultimately take possession of Canaan. Second, the allegorical interpretation: the soul, enslaved to sin (the fleshpots of Egypt), in the care of a great leader (Moses), endures many trials and temptations and at last wins through to salvation (the Promised Land). (One might refer to and summarize here other allegories the student might have encountered: the medieval play of *Everyman* and Bunyan's seventeenth-century *Pilgrim's Progress*.) Third, the moral interpretation, which might be simply put as "It matters what you do." When the Israelites followed God's laws, they found themselves moving on toward the goal; when they backslid, there were terrible punishments and delays. The fourth interpretation, the anagogical or mystical, needs—as a medievalist might say—no less than an angel to explain, but it might be suggested as a vision of darkness into light, or movement from a dangerous and barren wilderness into meaning, order, the New Jerusalem, and the soul's bliss. This last is what developed in Christian doctrine as the "typological" reading of the HB: Moses is a prototype of Christ, his holding up of the brazen serpent forecasts the crucifixion, and so on. For the students a review of this old fourfold method constitutes another suggestion of the importance of metaphor or the other-than-literal: the literal is limiting and misses a variety of possible values in the text. However, one can raise the issue of what legitimate literary criticism is: can we read a text out of its historical milieu and apply it to future events which the writer did not dream of? As religionists with a mystical view, yes; as literary critics we cannot. The typological reading, moreover, devalues what the HB is in its own right, as culture, as literature, and as religion.

An interesting tension between literal and metaphorical comes up in some of the Deuteronomic exhortations. When we read that the essential Mosaic Commandments are to be bound "for a sign upon thine hand, and they shall be as frontlets between thine eyes. And thou shalt write them upon the posts of thy house, and on thy gates" (Deut. 6:8–9), it might be imagined that this is an exhortation to act *as though* these commandments were marked on our hands, our foreheads, and our doorways. But pious Jews—students should be told—do actually write them on paper and put them in little containers that are then as phylacteries actually bound to the arm and forehead, and as mezuzoth actually attached to the doorposts. The actual practice, or literal interpretation, would not appear to be the essential thing, but is a symbol of the desired state of mind, the perpetual consciousness of the Commandments.

In the parts of the Bible that are poetry, metaphor becomes more than ever the mode of expression, and the Psalms, the Song of Solomon, Job, and the Prophets have enriched every culture they have touched, with a wealth of enduring figures. There are the great basic ones, of physical thirst for spiritual need ("As the hart panteth after the water brooks, so panteth my soul after thee, O God"—Ps. 42:1), of human life as grass, as the flower of the field (e.g., Ps. 37), the unique and charming children as arrows ("Happy *is* the man that hath his quiver full of them"—Ps. 127:5). Such figures become a special cultural resource. The *quiver*, for instance, yields rueful humor in Trollope's *Barchester Towers:* Mr. Quiverful is the clergyman who has so many children he cannot put high professional principle ahead of his duty to feed those many mouths. And then there are the extravagant cosmic celebrations of nature: the mountains that "skip like rams" and the "little hills, like lambs" (Ps. 114:6), or the "floods" that "clap their hands" (Ps. 98:9). Sometimes metaphor becomes wildly extravagant when challenged. Sexual experience is properly ineffable, and in the Song of Solomon the very extravagance of the figures is a confession of the failure of ordinary speech, and at the same time more evocative of that experience than one would have imagined. "I am the rose of Sharon, and the lily of the valley" becomes a statement of feeling. Good smells and tastes and textures are invoked, and there is great power of suggestion: "A garden enclosed is my sister, my spouse; a spring shut up, a fountain sealed." When the woman speaks of "our bed," she says "the beams of our house are cedar, and our rafters of fir"—which simply enacts the physical position of lying on your back, with characteristically brilliant Hebrew specificity.[4] Some metaphors catch the imagination as ever freshly as a figure from Dante or Shakespeare: "We spend our years as a tale *that is told*" (Ps. 90:9) speaks to a modern absurdist consciousness. "The heavens declare the glory of God" (Ps. 19:1) does not lose its meaning: the mute, inexpressibly beautiful expanse of stars above us is still *saying* something about the nature of existence. The figure is elegantly developed through the next five verses in suggestive analogy to ensuing verses on the beauty of the law, the nonmute verbalized wonder of the moral consciousness. The psalm is far from naive; it expresses in fact the two wonders of existence as Immanuel Kant saw them: the physical laws of the cosmos without, and the moral law within.

The study of metaphor becomes vital in a particular way in the poetic parts of the Bible because of the interplay between metaphor and structural parallelism. Quite habitually, sets of parallels will combine a metaphor in one stich with a discursive statement in the other.

Who shall ascend into the hill of the Lord	*a*
or who shall stand in his holy place?	*a*
He that hath clean hands,	*b*
and [he that hath] a pure heart	*b*
	(Ps. 24:3–4)

The pair of questions explain each other as referring to the temple sanctuary; in the pair of answers, the metaphorical "clean hands" is explained as a state of mind by the other metaphor of the "pure heart," which is so common as to have practically lost its metaphorical quality. In the chiastic *a b b a* of Psalm 51:1,

Have mercy upon me, O God a_1
 according to thy lovingkindness b_1
 according to the multitude of thy tender mercies b_2
blot out my transgressions, a_2

the "lovingkindness" of God in b_1 is explained delightfully as a "multitude of tender mercies" in b_2, and the particular mercy of a_1 is specified as the forgiveness of sins in a_2—still in a figure, *blotting out*.[5] The next couplet specifies still more, in two interglossing variants of a different figure:

Wash me thoroughly from my iniquity c_1
and cleanse me from my sin. c_2

It is only by appreciating these parallelisms that one can appreciate the metaphor:

The Lord is my shepherd; a_1
I shall not want a_2
            (Ps. 23:1)

This is so well known, one may no longer think about it. But in fact a_2 is a gloss on a_1. That is what it is to have the Lord for your shepherd—it is to be in need of nothing. From this sudden insight, one we can call (in a figure) *striking*, or *flashing*, the psalm proceeds in joy to list, in coordinate pairs, the complete series of wants, fulfilled completely. This poetic mode makes for extreme density and power.

With the Prophets, it would seem that metaphor is developed with the greatest virtuosity; there is even the conscious challenge of speaking of the Ineffable, as in this chiastic passage from Isaiah: The Lord speaks—

To whom will ye liken me   *a*
 and make *me* equal,   *b*

> and compare me,   *b*
> that we may be like?   *a*
>
> (Isa. 46:5)

And Hosea acknowledges metaphor as the definitive prophetic mode:

> I have also spoken by the prophets   *a*
>   and I have multiplied visions,   *b*
>   and used similitudes,   *b*
> by the ministry of the prophets.   *a*
>
> (Hos. 12:10)

And so the understanding of God develops through the HB with military metaphors—a fortress, a rock, a shield, a Lord of hosts; agrarian metaphors—a reaper, a winnower, a burning off of the stubble. He is an architect (Isa. 40:12), and the plumbline itself (Amos 7:7)—presumably standing for justice; a potter (Ps. 2:9, Isa. 30:14); and with the new technology of metalwork, he is a smelter (Isa. 1:25), a refiner's fire (Mal. 3:2). As retribution for evil, he is the besom (broom) of destruction (Isa. 14:23) or a razor (Isa. 7:20), and, recurrently, fire. God the Father is commonplace; Isaiah has an interesting figure of God as mother, as having borne Israel from the belly, from the womb (46:3), and again as a nursing mother whose full breasts keep her conscious of the child (49:15). Indeed, Phyllis Trible has argued that such figures disavow sexism in the biblical idea of God.[6] And out of the sheep-keeping economy come the great and beloved figures of God as "shepherd" (e.g., Ps. 23; Isa. 40:11) and of the suffering servant as the slaughtered lamb (Isa. 53:7). These figures run through all Western literature as enabling images, "aids to reflection," ready-made similitudes for poets.

The Book of Job has probably the most extended and astonishing metaphor of all in the Voice from the Whirlwind, which in a series of questions indicates the limits of human intelligence, and the unspeakable power that we cannot understand:

> Where wast thou when I laid the foundations of the earth?
> . . . .

When the morning stars sang together, and all the sons of
    God shouted for joy?

(Job 38:4–7)

In our sympathy with Job, we validate our own human sense of
justice—he *knows* his calamities are undeserved and he will not be
bullied into saying otherwise. At the same time through this metaphor of the Voice we are brought, like Job, to a condition of humility
and wonder in the face of the marvels of existence: the greatness of
nature, from the regularity of the cosmos, to the wonderful structure
of snowflakes, the mysteries of bird migration, the temperament of
the warhorse, to the working of the human mind, that too:

Who hath put wisdom in the inward parts?
or who hath given understanding to the heart?

(38:36)

It is one of the marvels of the self-conscious human mind that it can
be brought to realize its own limitations, and perhaps the most marvelous aspect of the human mind is the prodigious function of metaphor itself. Maybe no text in human history is more prodigious than
the Book of Job.

Sooner or later, one must bring up the phenomenon of anthropomorphism. The word itself is educative for the student who has not
met it before. "Man never knows how anthropomorphic he is," said
Goethe. But this study of metaphor in the Bible is an occasion to
consider just that, how human beings have in all cultures ascribed
human characteristics to the forces of nature. "Personification" em-
braces all such metaphors. The human—all too human—traits of the
God of the HB are characteristic: he walks in the cool of the evening,
he haggles with Abraham, he is susceptible to the flattery of Moses.
The more sophisticated ideas of God in Genesis 1 and Job 38 are still
of an entity that speaks in human language (*which* language, is an old
theological problem). Even sophisticated theologians, it might be
pointed out, are still anthropomorphizing when they talk of such
things as the "will" of God. It turns out to be virtually—I am tempted
to say absolutely—impossible to think about deity without metaphor.

Whether deity is in question or any other difficult matter—the
spiritual, the ethical, the unknown, the new attitude—the metaphori-

cal mode expresses it in terms of the known, the familiar, the visual-izable image, the physical sensation. Amos is a virtuoso. You feel secure, he says, but you are not. It is "as if a man did flee from a lion, and a bear met him; or went into the house and leaned his hand on the wall, and a serpent bit him" (Amos 5:19). You know what physical famine is, he says, and he gives the very *feel* of it, with a figure:

> I have given you cleanness of teeth in all your cities,
> and want of bread in all your places.
>
> (4:6)

There can also be a spiritual famine: "Behold, the days come, saith the Lord God, that I will send a famine in the land, not a famine of bread, nor a thirst for water, but of hearing the words of the Lord" (8:11). In the historical books, apostasy is sometimes referred to in the figure of adultery, of "whoring after strange gods." In Hosea, this figure becomes the master framing metaphor of the whole book. The marriage of Israel to God is desecrated by the apostasy of Israel—and the metaphor is compellingly developed in the hurt of the husband and his pained but forgiving and enduring love. Suitably enough, Hosea's incidental metaphors are housekeeping ones, of moths, of food going bad (5:12), of baking—Ephraim is a "cake not turned" (half-baked!—7:8). (Another notably domestic metaphor occurs in an incidental piece of doom prophecy in 2 Kings 21:13: "I will wipe Jerusalem as *a man* wipeth a dish, wiping *it*, and turning *it* upside down.") Agricultural images run through all these Prophets. Hosea develops one at some length:

> Sow to yourselves in righteousness,
> reap in mercy;
> break up your fallow ground:
> for *it is* time to seek the Lord,
> till he come and rain righteousness upon you.
> Ye have plowed wickedness,
> ye have reaped iniquity;
> ye have eaten the fruit of lies:
> because thou didst trust in thy way,
> in the multitude of thy mighty men.
>
> (10:12–13)

Isaiah is perhaps the richest and most varied. What Jeremiah calls "backsliding" (itself a metaphor from cattle raising, see Jer. 2:10 etc. and Hos. 4:16) Isaiah sees as the reversion of vineyard grapes, cultivated (by the Lord), to sour wild grapes (Isa. 5:2). This metaphor is developed at some length, as a parable, that short fictional genre which is to be characteristic of Jesus. The six verses of Isaiah's parable are followed by an explanation:

> For the vineyard of the Lord of hosts *is* the house of Israel,
> and the men of Judah his pleasant plant:
> and he looked for judgment
> but behold oppression;
> for righteousness,
> but behold a cry.
>
> (5:7)

The good crop is judgment and righteousness, but they have reverted to oppression and a cry. One of Isaiah's boldest figures comes when he appeals to his hearers in the voice of the huckster, hawking his wares as in an Eastern bazaar:

> Ho, every one that thirsteth
>   Come ye to the waters,
> and he that hath no money;
>   come ye, buy, and eat;
> yea, come, buy wine and milk
>   without money and without price.
>
> (Isa. 55:1)

Once again, a difficult spiritual idea is put into terms with which we are all too deplorably familiar, and we get the idea. Everywhere in . HB there is the cultivation of vivid appeal to the senses in powerful metaphors. Job wishes he had never been born, and laments in physical reference to childbirth, "Why did [not] the knees prevent me? Or why the breasts that I should suck?" (3:12). The Psalmist expatiates on the goodness of the Lord and exclaims, "O taste and see!" (34:8).

Out of this great Hebrew tradition of metaphor comes the new thing of Christianity, and yet in this literary respect of metaphor—as in others—it is close to its Hebrew roots. Isaiah, the most rich in metaphor, is of all HB books the one most quoted in the CB but is only one example of an "essential continuity," as W. D. Davies has called it. In recent scholarship, the CB, Davies points out, "has been increasingly re-Judaized"; Christianity is now considered to be not so much a new religion that superseded Judaism, but something that somehow perpetuates it.[7] The last five chapters of Mark alone—a scholar has calculated—have 57 quotations from the HB, 160 allusions, and 60 points of influence.[8] This in ten pages! This is intertextuality with a vengeance; indeed it would be hard to think of any text more intimately entwined with a preceding one.

In the Hebrew tradition, Jesus is a master of metaphor, and has even to teach its proper understanding. Nicodemus comes to him in his unregenerate literalism and says "How can a man be born when he is old? can he enter the second time into his mother's womb, and be born?" (John 3:4), and Jesus explains to him the working of the metaphor of being "born again." Similarly, he has to explain the metaphor of "living water" to the women of Samaria:

> Whosoever drinketh of this water shall thirst again: But whosoever drinketh of the water that I shall give him shall never thirst; but the water that I shall give him shall be in him a well of water springing up into everlasting life. (John 4:13–14)

The extended metaphor, or parable, becomes Jesus' characteristic teaching method. It can be defined as a short fiction with a surface meaning plus an ulterior meaning, saying an otherwise difficult thing in terms we can apprehend easily. Its most famous prototype is Nathan's story of the ewe lamb, in 2 Samuel 12. After David's unconscionable lapse in arranging the death of Uriah so that he himself might take Uriah's wife for himself, Nathan the prophet presents to him, the King, a case in which a man who had everything appropriated another's particularly beloved possession, the ewe lamb. David exclaims over the reprehensible deed, and Nathan turns to him saying, "Thou are the man!" By this means, David recognizes his own iniquity. And typically, in hearing a parable we make some moral discovery about ourselves. The form of Isaiah's parable of the vineyard (5:1–7) is frequently used by Jesus, even to the subsequent explanation or decoding, as with the parable of the seed and the sower (Matt. 13). "Without a parable spake he not unto them," says Matthew (13:34). But the incidental short metaphor is ubiquitous in Jesus' speech. He calls to him two fishermen, saying—not without humor— "I will make you to become fishers of men" (Matt. 4:19, Mark 1:17). He falls into this mode easily and naturally. At other times he is self-conscious, as in the innumerable occurrences of "Unto what shall I liken—" the Kingdom of God, this generation, whatever. Many of his metaphors are HB inheritances: Isaiah had exhorted us to "Arise, shine"; Jesus tells us to "Let your light so shine before men . . . " (Matt. 5:16). Many figures come from common domestic life: The apostles are the "salt of the earth" (Matt. 5:13); or they are the "leaven" in the dough representing how an idea can work to affect a whole society (Matt. 13:33, Luke 13:21); you don't present a culture with unassimilable concepts any more than you would patch an old garment with new cloth (Matt. 9:16). (What humble thrift in Jesus' hearers this suggests!) Agriculture, sheepherding, the kitchen yard give him the great concepts of the harvesting of the precious grain, or "bringing in the sheaves" of the saved souls (Matt. 3:37, John 4:35); or the basic concept of Jesus as shepherd—and we still have "pastors"; or the apostles as sheep among wolves (Matt. 10:16); or the mothering hen:

> O Jerusalem, Jerusalem, thou that killest the prophets, and stonest them which are sent unto thee, how often would I have gathered thy children together, even as a hen gathereth her chickens under her wing, and ye would not!

The *yoke* had been a figure for slavery in ancient times (Lev. 26:13) and recurs in Isaiah and Jeremiah; now Jesus turns it into paradox (and another elegant parallelism): "My yoke is easy, and my burden is light" (Matt. 11:30). Hypocrites are "whited sepulchres" (Matt. 23:27), beautiful outside, but inside, putrefaction. It is interesting that some important figures are drawn from the world of investment: there is the merchant and the "pearl of great price," or heaven, for which one would sell one's whole portfolio (Matt. 13:46); there is the parable of the talents, by which we find we must do what we can with the investment God has made in *us* (Matt. 25:14). (In fact, the

word *talent*, literally a coin, in its sense of natural ability, comes from
this text.) Then we are advised how to invest:

> Lay up not for yourselves treasures on earth, where moth and
> dust doth corrupt, and where thieves break through and steal:
> But lay up for yourselves treasures in heaven. . . . (Matt. 6:20)

There is always the weather, and we can all presage stormy days or
fair; but it might be still more important to presage the kind of moral
state to come. "O *ye* hypocrites, ye can discern the face of the sky;
but can ye not *discern* the signs of the times?" (Matt. 16:3). "Pearls"
can be religious truth:

> Give not that which is holy unto the dogs   *a*
> Neither cast ye your pearls before swine,   *b*
> lest they trample them under their feet   *b*
> and turn again and rend you.   *a*
>
> (Matt. 7:6)

Here again the chiastic parallelism elucidates the figure, the *pearls*
are *that which is holy; b b* concern the pigs, *a a* the dogs, and both
may be aliens or heathens, and the verse may be a proscription
against evangelizing the Gentiles.[9] Other figures are hardly tied to
any one culture: the blind lead the blind (Matt. 15:14); "straight is
the gate, and narrow is the way" (Luke 13:24); there is a whole
range of figures from bodily function to illuminate the spiritual life.
One critic notes:

> Men had come into the world, born of women: they must enter
> the Kingdom, born of God. They had life: they must have life
> eternal and abounding. They knew bodily hunger and thirst and
> weariness; but there was hunger and thirst and weariness of
> soul to be recognized and allayed. Worse than blindness, deaf-
> ness, dumbness, paralysis, and leprosy of the body, were blind-
> ness, deafness, dumbness, paralysis, and leprosy of the spirit.
> Death of the body they dreaded and evaded with all their power,
> but death of the soul they suffered without alarm or even con-

sciousness. Bondage to Rome galled them, but captivity to self
and sin gave them no concern. . . .[10]

With all these physical metaphors, the text touches us at many points
of our being; the intellectual purport of it is apprehended and also
felt in our senses, proved on our pulses.

It is remarkable that the gospel writers themselves are not particularly metaphorical at all, but bald, literal, often naive; while the
logia of Jesus that they have treasured up are charged with metaphor—vivid, vital, energized speech. Furthermore, it is a question
how much the old Hebrew convention of parallel structure was still
viable in Jesus' day. Matthew's ignorant misreading of Zechariah's
parallelism is notorious: "riding upon an ass, and upon a colt the foal
of an ass" (9:9), he understood to depict two animals, with very
awkward result: "And the disciples . . . brought the ass, and the colt,
and put on them their clothes, and they set him thereon" (Matt.
21)—*whereon?* on *both?* But Jesus himself often uses parallelistic style
in a way that would seem to indicate thorough awareness of its effectiveness—I have quoted some instances. Two further cases, however,
seem to me particularly characteristic and significant, in the interplay
of metaphor with parallels. When they brought to Jesus the man sick
with a palsy, he said to him "thy sins be forgiven thee," and the
scribes found this blasphemous. Jesus said to them, "Why reason ye
these things in your hearts? Whether it is easier to say to the sick of
the palsy, Thy sins be forgiven thee; or to say, Arise, and take up thy
bed and walk?" (Matt. 2:5–9). It would seem that these two alternates
are interglossing parallels: to have your sins forgiven you is to arise
and walk—the physical, once again, is a metaphor illuminating the
spiritual, and it is altogether in the HB tradition. In the "little Apocalypse" of Matthew 25, when the Son of Man has come into his Kingdom, he speaks to the saved:

> Come, ye blessed of my Father, inherit the Kingdom prepared
> for you from the foundation of the world: For I was an hungred,
> and ye gave me meat: I was thirsty, and ye gave me drink: I was
> a stranger, and ye took me in: Naked, and ye clothed me: I was
> sick, and ye visited me: I was in prison, and ye came unto me.
> Then shall the righteous answer him, saying, Lord, when saw
> we thee an hungred, and fed thee? or thirsty, and gave thee

drink? When saw we thee a stranger, and took thee in? or naked, and clothed thee? Or when saw we thee sick, or in prison, and came unto thee? And the King shall answer and say unto them, Verily I say unto you, Inasmuch as ye have done it unto the least of these my brethren, ye have done it unto me. (25:34–40)

The conclusion is a stunning pair of parallels that gather up the significance of Jesus' mission in a single metaphor: to do any of these good deeds to anyone is to serve God. (Whether *this* statement is literal or metaphorical is a question more for the theologian than the critic.)

Frequently, students should be invited to compare the KJV with other translations, and with versions in other languages if they have them. It will be observed that modern translations characteristically slight, or defuse, or at times even omit, the metaphor of the original, and that this frequently accounts for what is felt to be the failure of the NEB, for instance, "as literature." But it is really a failure in meaning. Gerald Hammond observes:

> Many modern versions eschew anything that smacks of imagery or metaphor—based on the curious assumption, I guess, that modern English is an image-free language. When Christ, in the Sermon on the Mount, talks about those who *hunger* and *thirst* after righteousness, the Good News Bible drops the images of hungering and thirsting, and renders it "Happy are those whose greatest desire is to do what God requires."[11]

How flaccid it is, the new version, and how *uninteresting*! I believe myself that many modern translators have a feeling that metaphors are difficult to understand, and therefore these translators flatten the text into dull discursive prose. But the truth is that metaphors make matters *easy*, and that's what they're for, and that's why these great texts have lived. And it is to be insisted on that with very few exceptions these biblical metaphors are translatable, for they come out of common experience. Northrop Frye declared that "it is practically impossible for a translator to get them wrong."[12] I have argued in chapter 2 that the patterns of biblical parallelism have contributed greatly to the translatability of the text; and certainly the nature of biblical metaphor is another factor in this translatableness.

Finally, I think in a course on the Bible-as-literature one need make no great claim for what many theologians argue for now as the supremacy of metaphor in religious discourse.[13] The consistent attention to metaphor simply works by itself to suggest something like that. And if one has students write short essays on metaphor analysis, to try to state in nonmetaphorical language what the meaning or effect of the metaphor is, one need not tell them that what they are doing is anything as radical or heterodox (from some sectarian points of view) as "demythologization." In fact, in biblical parallelism the frequent coupling of literal and metaphorical by itself suggests the "demythologizing" approach. The appreciation of the little "fictions" of metaphor can lead to the appreciation of our great fictions, and they will be enhanced and valorized thereby. Merely to consider in a fairly disciplined way this remarkable phenomenon of biblical metaphor does by itself induce a much more sophisticated frame of mind than most students start with, a broader, more tolerant attitude to religion, and an immensely heightened appreciation of our great texts, both secular and spiritual.

Chapter 4

Waiting for Gödel: Or Hierarchy and the Book of Job

Trying to define yourself is like trying to bite your own teeth.[1] That is an insight from Eastern religion, and the phrasing is Alan Watts's. It is not a mathematical statement, but it has an analogous mathematical parallel—in the theorem called Gödel's. And the theorem suggests, I propose, some useful ways of thinking about literature. Gödel's proof I have to take on faith, and can do so pretty securely, for so far as I can find out it is a proof generally accepted by mathematicians, and indeed generally admired and acclaimed. The theorem can be put as follows: "it is impossible to prove that a logical system at least as complicated as arithmetic contains no concealed contradictions by using only theorems which are derivable within the system." Consequently, "To prove mathematics free from potential contradiction one must use principles outside mathematics, and then to prove that these new principles do not conceal contradictions one must use principles beyond them. The regress has no end—one has languages and meta-languages without limit."[2] Furthermore: "Gödel's results . . . establish . . . that mathematics cannot be formalized in one formal system. Some hierarchy of systems is necessary. . . . Since mathematics has often been regarded as the standard of rational knowledge, Gödel's theorem seems to acquire significance for the whole body of human knowledge." But we are warned against an indiscriminate extension of Gödel's findings:

> No doubt these results and other "limitation" results have revealed a new and somewhat unexpected situation insofar as formal systems are concerned. But beyond these precise and almost technical conclusions, they do not bear an unambiguous philosophical message. In particular they should not be rashly called

upon to establish the primacy of some act of intuition that would dispense with formalization.[3]

Far be it from the literary critic to move rashly or intuitively. We are thoroughly aware of the limitations of our own systems. Because we work with language we are acutely conscious of these limitations. Noam Chomsky, taking language as a "central aspect" of human intelligence, recurrently declares that the human mind may not be up to understanding how the human mind works. Like the mathematicians, he has come to "limitation results" in a study of grammar.

> Clearly, the rules and principles of this grammar are not accessible to consciousness in general, though some undoubtedly are. . . . The fact that the mind is a product of natural laws does not imply that it is equipped to understand these laws. . . . A significant gap, more accurately a yawning chasm—separates the system of concepts of which we have a fairly clear grasp, on the one hand, and the nature of human intelligence, on the other. . . . It is an interesting question whether the functioning and evolution of human mentality can be accommodated within the framework of physical explanation, as presently conceived, or whether there are new principles that emerge only at higher levels of investigation than can now be submitted to physical investigation.[4]

The problem is, as P. W. Bridgman says, "The brain that tries to understand is itself part of the world that it is trying to understand."[5] Is not the literary critic particularly aware of the problem, in the study of the staggering complexity of the way language works in texts? Do we not sometimes see how philosophers, rigorous logicians even, are embarrassed by unappreciated inadequacies of the linguistic system? When we insist on the cultural necessity for knowing a language other than one's native one, is it not because we know the need to get outside the system, to evaluate it by another system or systems, to discover thereby the provisional and relative character of language? And are we not aware of demonstrations in literature itself of the invalidation of systems and of the efforts to transcend them?

It seems to me that the Book of Job must be the *locus classicus* of the literary form of Gödel's theorem. There is its remarkable structure of the folktale framework, the meeting of God and Satan in heaven and a sort of cosmic wager on whether man can withstand adversity, and the classical test case: The best of men faced with the worst and most of calamities. The folktale framework guarantees our superior, informed position; as *we* see Job stricken and as we attend to the discourse of Job and the comforters, presenting a sample of the ways in which men verbalize the problem of suffering and try to articulate adequate worldviews, we actually know more than the actors. I think the poet exploits artistically the very naïveté of this folktale, with Satan playing the role of devil's advocate, of all things. Of course we know this is not the way things can be, a sort of informal reception in heaven and good-humored discussion with the Unknowable, and since we cannot know the way things are—as the whole poem asserts—this banal little fairy tale-myth-legend suggests how we must make do with inadequate, provisional epistemologies. And these may be the means to otherwise unattainable insights, which are themselves valid. It is fitting that the folktale framework, beginning and end, is in prose, and the great central main section all in verse. Even though banal then, the framework affords us the detached ironic perspective, and we are by suggestion already outside the system of formal logic functioning in the dialogues.

The formal logic of the dialogues is not so naive or banal. Of the comforters, Eliphaz is the one whose arguments we respect the most, and he is the most sympathetic; but even he fails in sympathy. He reproves Job for cursing the day of his birth, for God is nothing if not just. He, Job, had been so splendid in precept and example when his life was free of calamity, but now "it toucheth thee, and thou art troubled" (4:5). Eliphaz affirms his faith in God's justice, and—in painful irony—asserts "Happy *is* the man whom God correcteth" (5:17). Job, and we, know that he is not being "corrected"; in fact, we know that it is because he is innocent that he suffers. His friends cannot believe that he is innocent and he cries out, "Oh that my grief were thoroughly weighed, and my calamity laid in the balances together!" (6:1); and "To him that is afflicted pity *should be shewed* from his friend; but he forsaketh the fear of the Almighty" (6:14). Job is steadfast in lamenting the injustice and in searching for an explanation. The friends have shown no understanding. "Teach me, and I will hold my tongue: and cause me to understand where I have erred. How forcible are right words! but what doth your arguing reprove?"

(6:25). *I* have not lost moral judgment; I know iniquity from righteousness. But Eliphaz denies Job's power to know his own righteousness: "Shall mortal man be more just than God?" (4:17).

Bildad and Zophar are harder trials than Eliphaz. Bildad is a sort of Polonius, full of traditional proverb and platitude. To Bildad's conventional morality, virtue-is-rewarded-and-vice-is-punished, Job counters "How should man be just with God?"—that is, how should man *make deals* with God. "For *he is* not a man as I *am that* I should answer him *and* we should come together in judgment" (9:32). Zophar is the voice of the theological establishment: God is omniscient and man is limited: Therefore, repent and reform. We see that none of the comforters can know Job's suffering, nor know his innocence, which two facts invalidate the comforters' wisdom, sure though they are of it. The "wisdom of the race" in Bildad and religious platitude in Zophar are painfully inadequate, yet both are so arrogantly certain that Job is driven to sarcasm: "No doubt but ye are the people, and wisdom shall die with you. But I have understanding as well as you; I am not inferior to you: yea, who knoweth not such things as these?" (12:2–3). And the poet reaffirms the ironic distance with a technique now considered very modern, very *dernier cri*: at the very height of crisis Job cries out, "Oh that my words were now written! oh that they were printed in a book!" and then the sublime "For I know that my redeemer liveth" (19:23–25), *redeemer* we are told being more accurately translated as *vindicator*. It might be said the *book* the words are printed in, the book as we read it, is the vindicator; and the figure might be interpreted most cautiously as an assertion that man has a sense of ultimate justice.

The contradictions, the paradoxes, the anomalies of this system of intellectualizing man's predicament are made cumulatively more obvious and painful, till the poet in a great and memorable moment makes a shift in perspective, and takes us out of that intellectual system into a metasystem. The metasystem has been anticipated in the despairing words of Job himself: "Where shall wisdom be found? and where is the place of understanding? Man knoweth not the price thereof; neither is it found in the land of the living. . . . God understandeth the way thereof, and he knoweth the place thereof" (28:12–23). Job's own arguments, however respectable and noble in their integrity, fail nevertheless in their own logic: for instance, he condemns God's justice, and yet expects to receive ultimate acquittal from Him; he flees God and yet yearns for Him. Job, superior morally and intellectually to the friends, is probably less logical than they. Their positions are more defensible in propositional terms, and yet in the context of the poem we know Job is—if one may say so—*righter*. But all the arguments are canceled by the Voice out of the Whirlwind:

> Who is this that darkeneth counsel by words without knowl-edge? Gird up now thy loins like a man; for I will demand of thee, and answer thou me. Where wast thou when I laid the foundations of the earth? declare, if thou hast understanding. Who hath laid the measures thereof, if thou knowest? or who hath stretched the line upon it? Whereupon are the foundations thereof fastened? or who laid the corner stone thereof; when the morning stars sang together, and all the sons of God shouted for joy? (38:2–7)

The metasystem is demonstrated, the ineffable is presented, in a way, the way of symbol. The syntax itself, all question now, unan-swerable question, symbolizes the departure from discursive logic. One is reminded of Wittgenstein's "Unsayable things do indeed ex-ist" (*Tractatus* 6:522) and the severe last proposition of the *Tractatus*: "Whereof one cannot speak, thereof one must be silent." Compare Job now: "I will lay mine hand upon my mouth" (40:4). And so must the arithmetician, Gödel says, lay his hand upon his mouth at a certain point. The change is expressed figuratively in Job's statement, "I have heard of thee by the hearing of the ear, but now mine eye seeth thee" (42:5); the *ear* would here symbolize logic, and the eye that more immediate apprehension by which we *see* the limitation of the logical system and *see* by symbol the fact of hierarchy.

But we remember the logicians' warning: Gödel's theorem "should not be rashly called upon to establish the primacy of some act of intuition that would dispense with formalization." True. Mathematicians do still have a discipline. And it seems to me that one of the most moving things about the Book of Job is that it reserves dignity and integrity to the formalization, to man's power of logic. "How forcible are right words!" exclaims Job (6:25). Words *can* be "right." "Though he slay me, yet . . . I will maintain my own ways before him" (13:15). Neither the comforters nor the universe can bully him into saying what he knows is not true. He is innocent. There may be something like a concept of original sin in Job, but there is a denial of responsibility for it.

Here is the aspect of Job that has reminded so many of Sophocles' Oedipus.[6] Both Job and Oedipus are as good as man—being human—can be; and both are heroic in maintaining integrity before God and denying culpability. The symbol of *sight* as *insight* that Job concludes with is central to Oedipus along with the Apollo-light imagery. The artistic method is very different, chiefly in respect to dramatic irony. In Job, the superior knowledge of the spectator is only suggested at the beginning, and then as it were suppressed in the body of the work, only to be reconfirmed with the stunning shift into the whirlwind, the primitive outline suddenly illuminated with depth and meaning; whereas in *Oedipus* the double ironic view is insisted on throughout, exploited in every scene and in almost every speech. The irony of the two perspectives in itself implies two systems; and to be aware of two perspectives, two systems, is to recognize the necessity for a yet new perspective that correlates the two. And so the drama, being display, or spectacle, can put before our eyes a kind of paradigm of systems and metasystems. Kenneth Burke says irony is the perspective of perspectives.[7] The achievement of it immediately grants the existence of hierarchy. And so Job and *Oedipus* work out in something the same way. There is, as Bridgman says of Gödel's implications, "no end—one has languages and meta-languages without limit."

One can always keep moving up the hierarchy until one encounters the Unknowable. Yet it is one of the interesting peculiarities of the psyche (or language) that we can think even about the Unthinkable. Thomas Aquinas perhaps does it with the most elegance and virtuosity, in his definitions of God as what we cannot conceive of.[8] He makes the approach to the limits of human thinking from various directions, and by defining the limits succeeds in a sort of outline or linear silhouette of the Unthinkable. One may not be able to discourse in the metalanguage; the point is to conceive of its existence.

But this is very hard to do, abstractly. In our poor anthropological way, we find it much easier to think in terms of characters and stories. And so works like Job and *Oedipus* can make a difficult concept accessible to us. It is a recurrent literary function. A famous and influential instance is that "Dream of Scipio" with which Cicero ends his *De Republica* by taking us to a vantage point high among the spheres. And Chaucer makes use of this Ciceronian device in the *Troilus*. It is another supreme literary moment, when we are taken out of the system into a metasystem. The ascent into hierarchy casts a new and different light for Troilus and for us, on "this litel spot of erthe," and "in himself he lough. . . . " There is laughter in the last section of Job, too.[9]

Poets discover hierarchy in an endless variety of ways. Pope even begins the Argument to the *Essay on Man* with what sounds very like the basic theorem, "That we can judge only with regard to our *own system*, being ignorant of the *relations* of systems and things [Pope's emphasis]." Compare, again, Wittgenstein: "Whereof one cannot speak, thereof one must be silent." But poets do not stay silent; they depart, rather, from discursive logic into the area of symbol. Take Henry Vaughan with the "ring":

> I saw eternity the other night
> Like a great ring of pure and endless light.
>
> ("The World" [1650], 1–2)

The experience is ineffable, and so he reports it in this colloquial way, a sort of sublime inadequacy. But what he can and does do discursively is tell how things look once he has had that experience, how changed, and then at the end of the poem he circles back in imitation of the ring itself into a symbolic statement of the relevance of eternity to us. Wordsworth recognizes the same sort of process in those careful, beautifully cautious and guarded reports of the "sense sublime of something far more deeply interfused," the "joy of elevated thought."[10] *Elevated* is a very precise word here, I think, in the sense of Gödelian hierarchy. Probably Wordsworth's best declaration of metasystem is the climactic symbol at the end of *The Prelude*, when the climbers who must be absorbed in finding their footing in the mist and dark of Mount Snowden emerge at last above the clouds—or *Angst*—into the light of the mountaintop, where everything stands clear, and in different terms. The experience is an *emblem*, he says. In *Paradise Lost*, Milton's devils in Hell are parallel in a way to Job's comforters. They embroil themselves in the tough problems

Of providence, foreknowledge, will and fate,
Fixed fate, free will, foreknowledge absolute,
And found no end, in wandering mazes lost

. . . .

Vain wisdom all, and false philosophy.

(*Paradise Lost* 2:559–65)

But Milton, having invoked the Third Person of the Trinity as his muse, finds himself privileged with the perspective of God and knows true wisdom and true philosophy.

Finally I should like to suggest Arnold's *Empedocles on Etna* as the Victorian *locus classicus* of the Job-Gödel theorem.[11] It is abundantly clear that Empedocles is the victim of overintellectualization, that enervating "dialogue of the mind with itself,"[12] structurally parallel to the philosophical hassles of Job and the comforters, or to the laborious footsteps on Wordsworth's clouded mountainside, or indeed to Milton's devils "in wandering mazes lost." The statement of *Empedocles* is the richer for its two phases: one, the philosopher in society—Empedocles to Pausanias; and two, the philosopher in soliloquy—in each, the "slave of thought." The limitations of human thought, the ways of logic, are Empedocles' theme, his tragedy even:

We shut our eyes, and muse
How our own minds are made.
What springs of thought they use,
How rightened, how betrayed—

(1.2.327ff.)

We examine and consider our system and address the gods:

True science if there is
It stays in your abodes!

(a very distinct echo of Job) and

Man's measures cannot mete the immeasurable All.

(1.2.339–41)

But mind, but thought—
. . . Keep us prisoners of our consciousness,

And never let us clasp and feel the All
But through their forms, and modes, and stifling veils.

(2.345–54)

There is much in Arnold's *Empedocles* that is reminiscent of
Carlyle, especially in this Gödelian aspect. Arnold's "immeasurable
All" is in fact Carlyle's actual phrase in *Sartor*.[13] Remembering
Carlyle's mathematical bent, I think he would have liked Gödel's
theorem. For it is in a way his one great theme; lacking the proof, he
travails with a plenitude of variation to get the message out. And it
is as a result of a discrepancy—Carlyle's sure sense of the theorem,
and his inability to demonstrate it conclusively—that we have those
many loquacious volumes, all, as someone has said, in praise of
silence. "Speech is great, but silence is greater." "Logic is good, but
it is not the best." There are "things which Logic ought to know that
she cannot speak of,"[14] and so on, *passim et passim*. He recognized the
theme early, in *Characteristics*: "Metaphysics is the attempt of the
mind to rise above the mind; to envision and shut in, or as we say,
comprehend the mind."[15] His recourse to symbol, as explained in the
"Symbols" chapter of *Sartor*, becomes, I believe, Arnold's poetic
method, most conspicuously perhaps here in his *Empedocles*.

The songs of Callicles, then, interspersed as they are with Empedocles' discourses, function to keep us aware throughout of the
song-poetry-symbol mode; and again the two systems imply the
metasystem, whose spokesman is at the end Callicles himself, and
the last word is a hymn. But Empedocles does not ignobly die: he
makes his decision

Before the sophist-brood hath overlaid
The last spark of man's consciousness with words. . . .

(2.29–30)

And he defends his use of reason:

I have loved no darkness,
Sophisticated no truth,
Nursed no delusion,
Allowed no fear!

(2.400–403)

But the way out of human logic is Callicles' Apollo-hymn at the end. Arnold characteristically links poetry and religion here: Apollo the god of poetry leads his choir, "the nine." *Choir* suggests religion, but this choir consists of the nine muses, the secular muses of literature and the other arts. They supply a kind of secular saving "grace" to the end of the poem.

> First hymn they the Father
> Of all things; and then
> The rest of immortals,
> The action of men.
>
> The day in his hotness
> The strife with the palm;
> The night in her silence,
> The stars in their calm.
>
>   (2.461–68)

The end is the Arnoldian ideal of peace, rather than the Hebrew one of cosmic celebration, but the poem shows cognizance of Job. Job was of course enduringly interesting to Arnold, early in his life, and late, and consistently; and Arnold's other great biblical favorite, the Book of Isaiah, which he edited himself, with a sense of its rich symbolism, is acknowledgedly reminiscent of Job.

> For my thoughts are not as your thoughts, neither are your ways my ways, saith the Lord. (Isa. 55:8)

Job is so basic to *Empedocles* that one may detect a specific nostalgia for that literary moment "when the morning stars sang together and all the sons of God shouted for joy." It is the last soliloquy of Empedocles:

> And you, ye stars
> Who slowly begin to marshal,
> As of old, in the fields of heaven,
> Your distant, melancholy lines!
> . . . You too once lived:
> You, too, moved joyfully

> Among august companions,
> In an older world, peopled by Gods,
> In a mightier order,
> The radiant, rejoicing, intelligent Sons of Heaven.
>
> (2.276–87)

Although the terms are nostalgic, the moment is nevertheless invoked, and the Gödelian theorem is demonstrated again. *Quod erat demonstrandum*.

But that is not really the end of the matter; it is not finished. It is, as Gödel shows in the case of arithmetic, *essentially* incomplete. The principle of incompleteness may even seem uncomfortably ubiquitous, and although often nobly demonstrated, can seem commonplace. Take Pascal: the heart has its reasons, which reason cannot know.[16] Obviously. To think about reason at all is to discover its limitations and therefore to impose a new perspective, answerable to our sense of limitation of the single perspective. It is the recurrent function of art to impose the new perspective. Even to paint a Campbell's Soup can on a canvas, frame it and put it in an art gallery, makes us look at the subject in a new way, not in the context of What shall I buy? or What shall I have for lunch?, but in the context of What is the nature of this object insofar as it can be determined? "The work of art," declares Wittgenstein, "is the object seen *sub specie aeternitatis*."[17] But this is still more commonly conceived as the office of religion. To think of God is, in one sense, to conceive that our ordinary human idea of time and logic is not the only one there is. The spectator at Sophoclean tragedy is said to share the detached view of God, and both *Oedipus* and the Book of Job achieve, at the end, the God-perspective. Something parallel, however humble, is achieved by the Campbell's Soup painting. Lear, when he at last reaches the vantage ground, conceives of becoming *God's spy*.[18] This imposition of the new perspective may be what Arnold intimates as the common ground of religion and poetry.

There is a useful little book by Ernest Nagel and James R. Newman that helps to mediate between Gödel's rigorous world and the world of the layman, and it has some valuable "Concluding Reflections":[19]

> Gödel's proof should not be construed as an invitation to despair or as an excuse for mystery-mongering. The discovery that there

are arithmetical truths which cannot be demonstrated formally does not mean that there are truths which are forever incapable of becoming known, or that a "mystic" intuition (radically different in kind and authority from what is generally operative in intellectual advances) must replace cogent proof. . . . It does mean that the resources of the human intellect have not been, and cannot be, fully formalized, and that new principles of demonstration forever await invention and discovery. We have seen that mathematical propositions which cannot be established by formal deduction from a given set of axioms may, nevertheless, be established by "informal" meta-mathematical reasoning. It would be irresponsible to claim that these formally indemonstrable truths established by meta-mathematical arguments are based on nothing better than bare appeals to intuition.

Surely this is very prudently said. There is no reason to despair of our intellects, or to jump the gun in a race after the irrational. Truths we feel to be demonstrable are our ground and security. "How forcible are right words!" Certainly we must be as consistent, as formal, as possible, not permitting those mistakes or solecisms which offend logic. For indeed, the validity of the informal metasystemic discovery depends on the validity of the precedent formal reasoning that found its own limitation. Pascal's declaration of the claims of the heart is the more valid for his having started in mathematics, even in the probability calculations instigated by the practical exigencies of the gaming tables. Husserl's transcendental has value only for the precedent rigorous striving for the *purity* of his phenomenology.[20] Wordsworth's declaration of the sense-of-something-far-more-deeply-interfused is the more valid for the extreme care in the precedent psychological observations. Arnold's coming to rest in Callicles' hymn is significant just because, with Empedocles, he has exhausted the possibilities of the "dialogue of the mind with itself." And in the Book of Job, the Voice out of the Whirlwind is glorious and resonant, in good measure because of the precedent lengthy, widely exploratory, discursive, exhaustive rationalizations of the comforters, notorious in their failure. The Voice is an enfranchisement.

As our terms of discursive logic are perpetually modified by the accumulated total of human experience, by the ever-varying language available, and varieties of individuals in interplay with vari-

eties of cultures, Gödel's theorem would mean, as Nagel and Newman say, that "new principles of demonstration forever await invention and discovery." It indicates, they say, that "the structure and
power of the human mind are far more complex and subtle than any
non-living machine yet envisaged." And so the office of art, or the
office of religion, is never done. New principles of demonstration
forever await invention and discovery. And these new principles are
not valuable for their softness or "mystery-mongering," but for their
precision and specificity. We are right when we value specificity in
our poets. Keats, for instance, who so often thinks *new*, writes in a
letter:

> I go among the fields and catch a glimpse of a stoat or a field-
> mouse peeping out of the withered grass—the creature hath a
> purpose and its eyes are bright with it. . . . Even here though I
> am myself pursuing the same instinctive course as the veriest
> human animal you can think of—I am however young writing
> at random [not *quite!*]—straining at particles of light in the midst
> of a great darkness—. . . May there not be superior beings
> amused with any graceful, though instinctive attitude my mind
> may fall into, as I am entertained with the alertness of a stoat or
> the anxiety of a deer? (To George and Georgiana Keats, Feb.
> 14–May 3, 1819)

Gödel's own work, write Nagel and Newman, "is a remarkable example of complexity and subtlety"—of the human mind. I think the
work must be *graceful*, too, in Keats's sense, and bright with precision
and intellectual discipline. "It is an occasion," Nagel and Newman
conclude, not for dejection, "but for a renewed appreciation of the
powers of creative reason." It is an occasion, too, for a renewed
appreciation of the powers of the artistic imagination and of that
ancient biblical Book of Job that remains so dynamic a part of our
heritage.[21]

Chapter 5

Handel's English Masterwork

In this decadence of the twentieth century, the brawling religious sects maintain their divergent positions with passionate intensity, but for most people, God has disappeared long since, and society is secularized. Nonetheless there is a certain ritual regularly enacted that unites a remarkably broad cross section of English-speaking people. It is celebrated about the time of the winter solstice, or Christmas, or Hanukkah, and sometimes again in the spring, the time of general rebirth and Easter. It belongs to a genre developed almost single-handed by the German who became the most English of composers, George Frideric Handel, and it is an English institution: Handel's *Messiah*. In London in the 1740s, the Italian-style opera was losing its audience for various reasons, and Handel was responding to changing tastes, such as the new bourgeois English predilection for libretti in English and for subjects from the Bible. *Messiah* was tried out in Dublin under auspicious circumstances and then performed in a London theater in March of 1743. Audiences had accepted HB subjects in the theater, but *Messiah* seemed too sacred for secular surroundings, and it met with considerable hostility as blasphemous. On the other hand, it was not proper church music, and ecclesiastical authority objected to performances in churches. In time, Handel took to conducting it for charity in the Foundling Hospital Chapel, and it began to find its audience, which grew steadily through the eighteenth century and also through the nineteenth century, when the number of performers likewise grew, to the cast of thousands (three or four thousand) in the overblown Crystal Palace Exhibition performances of 1859 which George Eliot and everybody else attended.[1] And the audience has gone on growing through the twentieth century so that now *Messiah* sing-alongs draw big crowds; there are enough people around, that is, who own a dog-eared score and once sang it at school or church, to fill the auditoriums and join in the choruses with thunderous gusto. For many, *Messiah* appears to be a more acceptable religious ritual than a church service. It is at the same time much sung in churches. Certainly the long flourishing English tradition of choral performance has helped to keep it well known. But above all, while so much great vocal religious music is in Latin, and so much vocal music in general is in Italian or German or French, no doubt a great drawing power of *Messiah* is that it is in English. In fact, of all "serious" vocal music, *Messiah* may well be the most sung and best known throughout the English-speaking world. Furthermore, and this also accounts for its power, the text is a literary masterpiece. All of it is drawn from the King James Bible or the Prayer Book Psalter, and the selection and arrangement of the texts is done with consummate art. The result is that this particular collection of verses may be said to constitute the best known parts of the Bible. It is the great music that has made it so known, but text and music coexist in that symbiotic relationship that marks the greatest vocal music. The text, though, is generally taken for granted. But surely it is an extraordinary piece of literature, worthy of close analysis.

Its development is part of the history of music, well studied by Handel scholars; but it is also part of English literary history. Ever since Sir Philip Sidney had cited three great incidental poems of the HB, the Songs of Moses, of Miriam, and of Deborah, as examples of the world's first poetry, and he himself and his sister the Countess of Pembroke had done distinguished translations of the Psalms, there was a steady stream of biblical paraphrase and translations. Milton and Pope, to name the most famous, did psalm translations. The challenge is to make over the Hebrew into English verse, with English meter and English rhyme; and of course all these translations therefore put at risk, or lose, the translatable parallel patterns of Hebrew poetry. The secular critic might conclude that it was a good thing for literature that the KJV "prose" translation remained sacred, or at least "authorized to be used in churches," for in it was preserved the real parallelistic poetry of the Hebrews. There was, on occasion in England, praise for Hebrew poetry, but it was mostly piously vague. Addison did intimate something of its quality and even its translatableness: he exclaimed, "How kindly the Hebrew manners of speech mix and incorporate with the English language!"[2] Pope wrote a "Messiah, A Sacred Eclogue in Imitation of Virgil's Pollio," 1712;[3] a poem of 108 lines in heroic couplets, based on Isaiah's predictions. In a comparatist vein he appends in notes similar passages from Virgil's Fourth Eclogue with its famous predictions "Jam redit et Virgo . . . " and gives his own prose translations, his aim being to show how "the images and descriptions of the Prophet are superior to those of the Poet." Whether Pope is superior to the KJV Prophet, the reader may judge:

Ye Nymphs of Solyma [Jerusalem]! begin the song . . .
A Virgin shall conceive, a Virgin bear a Son!
From Jesse's Root behold a Branch arise,
Whose sacred Flow'r with Fragrance fills the Skies. . . .

At any rate, these biblical imitations were so common as to constitute a veritable genre, the "Religious Sublime."

Old Testament narrative was increasingly appreciated for its excitement and dramatic characters as well as for edification, and there were some signs of impatience with pious typological interpretation. And there was a further interest: it was found that you could make political statements by clever retelling of HB events: Dryden's *Absalom and Achitophel* (1681), with all its ingenuity and wit, is only the most famous of many examples. This kind of codification remains a resource for the ingenious. Verdi was able in his *Nabucco* to rally with impunity the Italian sentiment against the Austrian oppressor by depicting the Babylonian captivity and the great choral call for revolt. In eighteenth-century England this very useful form of HB history was widely exploited. Handel himself in his *Judas Maccabeus* celebrates the Duke of Cumberland's victory at Culloden. The general English predilection for the HB took shape, then, in this political sense at the same time as the "Religious Sublime" was cultivated, and both trends come together in the work of Charles Jennens, librettist of *Messiah*.

Jennens was one of those who early recognized Handel's creative genius; he became a passionate (but not uninformed) devotee and attended all available performances. This surely ought to predispose us in his favor. In a way Handel's reputation has suffered from the popularity of *Messiah*, to obscure his tremendous range of achievement. Jennens had a vision of combining the greatest texts of all with the greatest music of all. And it is a creditable vision, one that survives examination in modern times. The oeuvre is enormous and enormously varied and is now, it might be said, coming into its own. The Handel revival, begun in prewar Cambridge, promoted by Winton Dean's scholarship, is now part of the ever more lively early music movement. It reveals a composer who justifies Haydn's and Beethoven's worship of him. As for the text, it has stayed wonderfully accessible, just as the KJV has remained the most beloved Bible version. And it has none of the problems present-day audiences encounter with stilted eighteenth-century libretti.

Handel had first come to England in 1708, after promising beginnings in Germany and Italy, and quickly became acclimated and successful. His Hanoverian connections at court helped, but there was also a thoroughgoing recognition of his genius. In 1713 he was granted a pension by Queen Anne and commissions for English church music and ceremonial music, and in 1715 the new king, the Hanoverian George I, doubled his pension. He adopted a more or less English spelling for his name, George Frideric Handel. In 1727 he became a citizen of England by act of Parliament. He established himself in his great anthems, mostly settings of English psalms, but his overriding interest was Italian opera, which was the rage. Wilfred Mellers describes the situation:

> When cosmopolitan Handel settled in England it was partly with the intention of selling *opera seria*, the central artistic convention of his Heroic Age, to our increasingly affluent middle class. In commercial terms he failed, perhaps because the commonsensical British agreed with Dr. Johnson that opera was "an Exotick and Irrational Entertainment." But Handel was not defeated; craftily, he adapted the traditional operatic themes and techniques to create English oratorio, wherein the traditional conflict between private passion and public duty, and between self-vaunting ego and fallible human nature, was geared no longer to classical mythology, but to the merciless ethics of the Old Testament, the book Britishers knew best and relished most.[4]

As early as 1718, he had set English texts to music for the stage, in the masque with a classical subject, *Acis and Galatea*. But by 1732 he was dealing steadily with English libretti and HB subjects. *Esther*,

1732, was an adaptation of Racine's play, first performed privately and then when in the opera house done in the style of an oratorio, the Bishop of London apparently insisting there should be "no Action on the Stage," because of its sacred subject.[5] There followed *Deborah* in 1733, and *Athalia* soon after. All three exploit the sensational dramatic riches of the HB as well as affording showcases for star female voices: the adventures of Esther at the Persian court and how she saved her people, the story of Deborah and Jael and Sisera (this one was not so successful—perhaps the murder was *too* grisly), and the overthrow of the tyrant queen Athalia, daughter of the monstrous Jezebel. He continued to compose music for English words: Dryden's *Alexander's Feast* and *Ode for St. Cecelia's Day*, Milton's *L'Allegro* and *Il Penseroso* (to which the librettist Charles Jennens added a section on the moderate man *Il Moderato*, someone in between Milton's two extremes). But his biblical subjects continued, with *Saul*, 1739, libretto by Jennens, using the Bible (1 and 2 Sam.) as well as Cowley's *Davideis*; *Israel in Egypt*, 1739, libretto probably also by Jennens, from Exodus 15 and the Prayer Book Psalter. He seems to have continued to hope for success in Italian opera, but in 1740 his last ones, *Imeneo* and *Deidamia* failed, and the future seemed to point to the oratorio. In 1741 he was invited to Dublin and there premiered with triumphant success his new work *Messiah*, on the text arranged by Jennens. On his return to London, his *Samson*, adapted from Milton, was well received and did much to establish his future with English librettos, English singers, and an increasingly middle-class audience rather than the *beau monde* which had had a rage for Italian opera. The eternally rising middle class, however, had its leanings toward Evangelicalism, Methodism, and Puritanism, and where the HB narrative subjects had been acceptable in the theater, *Messiah* cut closer to the bone, treating the most sacred mysteries, and so it was that when it was performed at Covent Garden it was felt to be blasphemous. The new Foundling Hospital, supported by royalty and fashion, had received a splendid new chapel, and to inaugurate it in 1750 Handel arranged a charity performance of *Messiah*. This was the perfect solution, raising money for the hospital and attracting an enthusiastic audience; these performances became an annual occurrence, and *Messiah* was increasingly acclaimed and loved.[6] Thereafter there was a steady stream of oratorios: *Semele, Joseph and His Brethren, Hercules, Belshazzar* (Jennens as librettist again), *Judas Maccabeus, Joshua,*

Alexander Balus (from 1 Macc.), *Susanna, Solomon, Theodora,* and *Jephtha.* In this array of oratorios only two are classical, and of the others only *Theodora* is not biblical—it is the story of a Christian martyr of the fourth century. The rest are all taken from the HB narrative—or HB Apocrypha (Maccabees, Susanna). But *Messiah* is a great exception: it is the only one of all to use CB material, and the narration encompasses the whole Christian message. The CB material, however, is not so preponderant as it might seem: even the most Christian-sounding passages are in HB terms—Isaiah, Psalms, and those parts of Isaiah and Psalms quoted or alluded to in the Gospels and Epistles.

"The oratorios can never be understood without a careful study of the words as well as the music," declared Winton Dean, foremost of Handel scholars.[7] But this study has been surprisingly slow to come, even in the case of this most famous oratorio of all. To study the libretto, we need to study the librettist, Charles Jennens, and he has only just emerged from the evil report of history through the scholarly work of Ruth Smith.[8] The truth is, he was a Shakespeare scholar and editor of rare distinction, and therefore reviled by the jealous George Steevens, inferior Shakespeare editor, and it is Steevens's calumny that stuck to him, enshrined even in the *Dictionary of National Biography* (DNB) Jennens entry, which makes him out to be parvenu and simpleminded. He was in fact a man with aristocratic connections who moved comfortably among the great; he was broadly learned in literature and music and art, a great collector and a great patron.

He was also, Ruth Smith writes, a man of passionate loyalties: his "activities as squire, connoisseur, patron, author and friend were underpinned by two deeply held allegiances, religious and political: to Protestant Christianity and to the deposed English royal family, the house of Stuart."[9] He was never suspected of treason, but he supported the Stuart cause insofar as it was legal to do so and was a leader and patron of the Nonjurors, that party which sacrificed certain civil and ecclesiastical rights to principle, refusing to swear allegiance to William and Mary as usurpers of the Stuart line felt to have divine right. The Nonjurors were as a group outstandingly devout Anglicans, strong for the revival of earlier liturgies, and for the significance of the Eucharist; in fact they are considered to anticipate the Tractarian Movement of the nineteenth century. Nonjurors could nevertheless be faithful members of the Established Church, which they saw threatened on the one hand by Dissenters and on the other hand by the Deists. The Deists, one remembers, believed in a supreme Creator—and little else. Primary Deist texts reveal their bias in their titles: Locke's *Reasonableness of Christianity* (1695) and Toland's *Christianity Not Mysterious* (1696). Anthony Collins's *Discourse on Free-thinking* (1713) was further yet away from orthodox supernaturalism, and his later *Discourse on the Grounds and Reasons of the Christian Religion* (1724) derides the miraculous and denies that the HB contains prophecies of Christ.[10] The Deist debate raged loud and strong through the period of Handel's career, with plentiful polemics on both sides. Charles Jennens was a leader of the anti-Deist party.

Having the discernment to recognize Handel's stature, he attached his causes to Handel's star. There is no question that *Messiah* was his idea. He chose "passages from the Bible stating the fundamentals of Christian faith, to be promulgated by the greatest composer of the day—in *Messiah*, a work which he initiated."[11] He was intensely committed to the project, and it transpires that the texts he chose were in large part among those involved in the Deist controversy.[12] He hoped, he said, that Handel would "lay out his whole Genius and Skill" on the work; "he [Handel] said he would be a year about it, and make it the best of all his Compositions." Handel, however, was in one of those astounding phases of white heat, and completed the setting in little more than three weeks. Jennens was offended, as though Handel had "tossed off" something. "I shall put no more Sacred words into his hands to be thus abused."[13] It is true that Handel adapted for *Messiah* passages from some of his secular Italian music,[14] and Jennens, knowing Handel's music well, might have found this offensive where we would not. He badgered Handel about details, and Handel seems to have taken it in good part. Jennens carefully saw to the revision of the hastily printed Dublin text. Handel in the Dublin performance had omitted the chorus "The Lord gave the word; great was the company of the preachers," and it seems that it was at Jennens's insistence that it was restored for the London performance, it being a text that would endorse the Nonjurors' emphasis on the missionary effort. In the earlier *Saul*, Jennens had demanded alterations that emphasize the doctrine of the divine right of kings and that quote the passages that were part of the service for the Feast of King Charles the Martyr (2 Sam. 1),[15] the favorite saint of the Nonjurors. After *Messiah,* Jennens did not initiate any more settings of scripture. But Handel had it in mind to do *Belshazzar* and now was in the position of having to persuade Jennens to compose the libretto. Jennens complied, seeing, no doubt, another opportunity to wed great art with theological correctness. As he himself put it, he was ready "to make use" of Handel.[16] In *Belshazzar,* as in *Saul* and *Messiah,* Jennens's ideology is clear: the Daniel material is used so as to emphasize the predictions of Christ and the figure of Daniel as a "type" of Christ. This is of course the traditional Christian interpretation, especially endorsed by the Nonjurors.[17]

Some time before Ruth Smith's revelation of Jennens's role in *Messiah,* Geoffrey Cuming in an article of 1950 demonstrated that nearly all the text of *Messiah* is straight out of the Book of Common Prayer in its Revision of 1662.[18] Cuming quotes an earlier critic praising as original the "felicitous combination" of Job and 1 Corinthians in part III, "I know that my Redeemer liveth," with "For now is Christ risen . . . , Behold I tell you a mystery"; and he points out that the combination is hardly original but simply the time-honored one of the Anglican Burial Service. Cuming has a lively admiration of the libretto and cannot believe that the Jennens of the DNB could have composed anything so good; he inclines to give Handel himself a good deal of the credit. This is not fantastic. Handel was very familiar with the English Bible and had shown an excellent literary sense in his settings already. When Queen Caroline died, the Bishop of London offered his services to Handel for the selection of texts for the funeral anthem, and Handel gave him a firm rebuff, saying he was a great reader of the Bible himself and perfectly able to choose.[19] But here he settled for Jennens's choices and arrangements.

Let us examine, then, this interesting text. I follow Burrows's numbering of sections, and for the words themselves I use the old edition of Chrysander's,[20] but there are virtually no variations in the words. The "original" *Messiah* is, of course, notoriously problematic, there being no less than nine authoritative versions, for Handel himself adjusted the performances to accommodate varying resources.[21] (This fact makes performances very convenient: directors can have legitimate options according to the resources at hand.) The text is the constant, except that we know the Dublin performance omitted "the Lord gave the word," which was restored in ensuing performances at Jennens's instance. I have found, otherwise, only one variant, very minor: Burrows prints "If God is for us" where the other editions have the KJV subjunctive, "If God be for us."

And now to consider the text itself. First, listeners and performers who examined the title page of the Word Book[22] would receive clues as to the nature of Jennens's project. For there is the Latin motto printed under the title *Messiah: Majora Canamus*. It comes from the well-known opening of the Fourth Eclogue of Virgil, supposed since medieval times to predict the birth of Christ. "Sicelides Musae, paulo maiora canamus"; in the old translation, "Sicilian Muses, let us sing a somewhat loftier strain." Virgil turns from pastoral poetry to predicting the birth of a son to his friend and patron the consul Pollio. Modestly he says *paulo majora*, things a *little* greater, but Jennens is suggesting we sing now of unequivocally greater things, things spiritual not secular. Then there is an epigraph:

> And without controversy, great is the mystery of godliness: God was manifested in the flesh, justified by the Spirit, seen of angels, preached among the Gentiles, believed on in the world, received up into glory. In whom are hid all the treasures of wisdom and knowledge.

The first sentence, from the end of 1 Timothy 3, epitomizes with remarkable concision the whole Christian message that is the substance of the whole of *Messiah*. The second sentence, Colossians 2:3, expresses Jennens's unequivocal view that all pagan learning is as nothing compared with Christianity. On one occasion, for instance, he had said he was "grieved to find a Man of Parts neglecting his Bible for Heathen Philosophy."[23] So we have at the very start a clear indication of how Jennens viewed this undertaking. And now for the text proper, and some observations on Jennens's art.

Word Book

SINFONY

PART I

1. ACCOMPAGNATO

Isaiah 40:1   Comfort ye, comfort ye my people, saith your God.

Isaiah 40:2	Speak ye comfortably to Jerusalem, and cry unto her, that her warfare is accomplished, that her iniquity is pardoned: . . .
Isaiah 40:3	The voice of him that crieth in the wilderness, Prepare ye the way of the Lord, make straight in the desert a highway for our God.

2. ARIA

Isaiah 40:4	Every valley shall be exalted, and every mountain and hill . . . made low: . . . the crooked . . . straight, and the rough places plain:

3. CHORUS

Isaiah 40:5	And the glory of the Lord shall be revealed, and all flesh shall see it together: for the mouth of the Lord hath spoken it.

It must be one of the most felicitous openings for any piece of vocal music, to have that annunciatory tenor[24] stand up to sing this sequence from Isaiah, to proclaim with serene assurance that there is now an end of tribulation. Here it is indeed as though he *arises*, and *shines*, to borrow another phrase from Isaiah. This choice of opening text is in itself a brilliant stroke of Jennens. The verses are deftly adjusted: the ellipsis after "pardoned" marks the omission of "for she hath received of the Lord's hands double for all her sins," which happens to contain an interpretive problem and raise difficulties in comprehension and is therefore wisely omitted. The ellipses in section 2 represent only the omission of *shall be, and*, and *shall be made*— connectives made unnecessary by the economy of the setting. Verse 3 preserves the KJV mistranslation that the Gospels apply to John the Baptist in the wilderness; in the original the voice cries a parallel couplet: "In the wilderness prepare . . . , make straight in the desert . . . ," but thanks to the Gospels, the voice crying in the wilderness has become a commonplace in English, and here it is effective dramatically and rhetorically.

4. ACCOMPAGNATO

Haggai 2:6	. . . thus saith the Lord of hosts; Yet once, . . . a little while, and I will shake the

heavens, and the earth, ... the sea, and
the dry land;

Haggai 2:7   And I will shake all nations, and the desire of all nations shall come: ...

Malachi 3:1   ... the Lord, whom ye seek, shall suddenly come to his temple, even the mes-
senger of the covenant, whom ye delight
in: behold, he shall come, saith the Lord
of hosts.

5. ARIA

Malachi 3:2   But who may abide the day of his coming? And who shall stand when he ap-
peareth? For he is like a refiner's fire, ...

6. CHORUS

Malachi 3:3   ... and he shall purify the sons of
Levi, ... that they may offer unto the Lord
an offering in righteousness.

These passages from Haggai and Malachi are associated by the logic
of narrative with the preceding verses, and indeed are associated
with Isaiah by long tradition. They fulfill the expectation of the stupendous events announced in the preceding. Haggai's *a little while* is
suggestive moreover of the CB; the phrase runs like a refrain through
the gospel of John. Again, the ellipses in Haggai 2:6–7 effect a fine
economy: in 2:6, *For, it is,* and *and* are omitted, and in 2:7 the last
half of the verse: "and I will fill this house with glory, saith the Lord
of hosts." The first half of Malachi 3:1 is likewise omitted as restating
something like Isaiah 40:3. The turn from Malachi 3:1 to Malachi 3:2,
from the drama of recitative to the meditative aria, poignant in the
original text, is well exploited by both Jennens and Handel. It is a
turn from a cataclysmic event to the consequent soul-searching, to
fear and trembling: Who may abide these things! For the ways of God
are terrible: he is like a refiner's fire. Jennens did not complete the
verse—with particularly good reason, for the KJV reads "he is like a
refiner's fire, and like fuller's soap"! A fancier of Hebrew parallelism
should regret the omission of the second element, the soap, and
indeed the metaphor of *cleansing* is frequent and dignified in the
Bible, but one cannot but think the *soap* here would be a disaster, and
Jennens knew it. The *refiner's fire* is a magnificent image by itself for

God's processes, used before Malachi by Isaiah (1:25 and 48:10). Malachi 3:3, likewise wisely cut to essentials, follows with a fine logic: *like a refiner's fire, he shall purify.* The "sons of Levi" refers of course to the priesthood; by this figure the librettist can recommend the reform of the Anglican Church, discreetly and without offense.

7. RECITATIVE

Isaiah 7:14   . . . Behold, a virgin shall conceive, and bear a son, and shall call his name Immanuel, "God-with-us."

8. and 9. ARIA AND CHORUS

Isaiah 40:9   O thou that tellest good tidings to Zion, get thee up into the high mountain; O thou that tellest good tidings to Jerusalem, lift up thy voice with strength; lift it up, be not afraid; say unto the cities of Judah, Behold your God!

With section 7, Jennens returns to Isaiah and the famous contested passage. As Nonjuror, he stood by Isaiah's prediction in about 600 BCE of the birth of Jesus by the Virgin Mary, which the Deists and certain scholars considered nonsense. He omits the opening "Therefore the Lord himself shall give you a sign" and adds "God-with-us" from Matthew 1:23, one of the numerous places in the CB which quote Isaiah. The effect is to conflate HB with CB, in accord with his views, and, of course, in accord with orthodoxy. Isaiah 7:14 is part of the Christmas Day morning service. With the next section, Isaiah 40:9, he makes slight changes, from "O Zion, that bringest good tidings, get thee up into the high mountain; O Jerusalem, that bringest good tidings . . . ," which certainly make better sense and better sound. It speaks for Jennens's effectiveness that the *Messiah* version of this verse will sound to many ears more authoritative and familiar than the KJV.

Isaiah 60:1   Arise, shine, for thy light is come, and the glory of the Lord is risen upon thee.

10. ACCOMPAGNATO

Isaiah 60:2   For, behold, . . . darkness shall cover the earth, and gross darkness the people: but

the Lord shall arise upon thee, and His
glory shall be seen upon thee.

Isaiah 60:3   And the Gentiles shall come to thy light,
and kings to the brightness of thy rising.

Isaiah 60:1–3 plays on the great metaphor of light, as knowledge, relief from darkness, salvation, starting with *Arise, shine,* a remarkable individualizing and personalizing of the image: by the *thy*, I am admonished to shine; then in 2 is envisaged the people, and the light extending to them through the individual; and in 3 the light extends still further, to the world. The ellipsis in Isaiah 60:2 indicates the omission only of *the*. All three verses, 60:1–3, are part of the Evensong Service for Christmas Eve.

11. ARIA

Isaiah 9:2   The people that walked in darkness
have seen a great light: and they that dwell
in the land of the shadow of death, upon
them hath the light shined.

12. CHORUS

Isaiah 9:6   For unto us a child is born, unto us a son
is given: and the government shall be
upon his shoulder: and his name shall be
called Wonderful, Counsellor, The Mighty
God, The Everlasting Father, The Prince
of Peace.

Here the librettist maintains the imagery of light by switching from chapter 60 to 9, and in a beautiful parallelism the people that walked in darkness are identified as those that live in the shadow of death— which means all of us. And then in 9:6, the cause, or First Cause, is identified and celebrated in the magnificent series of appositives. These two passages are used in Christmas Day matins. The *and* in 9:2 seems to be added for musical rhythm.

13. PIFA (Pastoral Symphony)
14. RECITATIVE

Luke 2:8   . . . there were . . . shepherds abiding in
the field, keeping watch over their flock
by night.

Luke 2:9	And, lo, the angel of the Lord came upon them, and the glory of the Lord shone round about them: and they were sore afraid.
Luke 2:10	And the angel said unto them, Fear not: for, behold, I bring you good tidings of great joy, which shall be to all people.
Luke 2:11	For unto you is born this day in the city of David a Saviour, which is Christ the Lord.
Luke 2:13	And suddenly there was with the angel a multitude of the heavenly host praising God, and saying,

15. CHORUS

| *Luke 2:14* | Glory to God in the highest, and peace on earth, good will towards men. |

After the pastoral, or shepherd, music, at last in section 14, the soprano, withheld in most performances till now, begins to a star-twinkling string or sometimes harpsichord accompaniment the CB narrative from Luke, the best loved version of the Christmas story. It is carried through to verse 14, omitting only verse 12, "And this shall be a sign unto you. . . . " These verses are the reading for matins on Christmas Day. The omissions in 2:8 are *And*, and *were in the same country*. In 2:14, the KJV reads *and on earth peace*, which is reversed here to normal order.

16. ARIA

| *Zechariah 9:9* | Rejoice greatly, O daughter of Zion; shout, O daughter of Jerusalem: behold, thy King cometh unto thee: he is the righteous Saviour, . . . |
| *Zechariah 9:10* | . . . and he shall speak peace unto the heathen: . . . |

The Zechariah passages are quoted in the gospel for the first Sunday in Advent, Luke 19:38. Verse 9 omits from Zechariah, discreetly, *lowly, and riding upon an ass, and upon a colt the foal of an ass;* for this is a passage of Hebrew parallelistic poetry, where *colt* is in apposition to *ass*, famously misunderstood in Matthew 21:2–7 to mean two separate animals. *He is just and having salvation* is boldly changed to a more dramatic, and clearer, *he is the righteous Saviour*. Verse 10 omits the opening lines on disarmament, *I will cut off the chariot from Ephraim, and the horse from Jerusalem, and the battle bow shall be cut off,* which with its antique diction might deflect from the important point of the speaking of peace.

17. RECITATIVE

Isaiah 35:5   Then shall the eyes of the blind be opened, and the ears of the deaf . . . unstopped.

Isaiah 35:6   Then shall the lame man leap as a hart, and the tongue of the dumb shall sing: . . .

This is one of those Isaiah passages self-consciously fulfilled in the gospel, e.g., Matthew 11:5. There are some minor changes, as of word order for dramatic effect: *Then shall* in both verses instead of *Then the eyes of the blind shall be opened,* etc.; *an hart* becomes *a hart.* The ellipsis in 6 represents the omission of *waters breaking out in the desert;* the librettist may figure that there have been enough miracles, and waters breaking out is less attractive anyway in wet England than in dry Palestine.

18. ARIA

Isaiah 40:11   He shall feed his flock like a shepherd: and he shall gather the lambs with his arm, and carry them in his bosom, and . . . gently lead those that are with young.

Here the librettist returns to the chapter of Isaiah used in the opening sections, understood to present the prototype of Jesus as the good shepherd, self-consciously fulfilled by Jesus himself referring to Isaiah: "I am the good shepherd" (John 10:14). It is sung usually as a soprano and contralto duet, one of the tenderest and loveliest of songs, for this tender and loving image. The *and* in line 1 is an interpolation; a *shall* is omitted before *gently.*

Matthew 11:28	Come unto Him, all ye that labour and are heavy laden, and He will give you rest.
Matthew 11:29	Take His yoke upon you, and learn of Him, for He is meek and lowly of heart: and ye shall find rest unto your souls.

19. CHORUS

Matthew 11:30	... His yoke is easy, and His burthen is light.

These lines, very familiar to churchgoers as the first of the "Comfortable words" in the Communion Service, embody what is surely one of the most appealing aspects of Christianity to heavy-laden humanity. Jennens has made a very significant adjustment to the lines: *Come unto me* in the KJV is changed to *come unto Him* and the ensuing pronouns changed accordingly. For one thing, this change makes the line consistent with the third person of the preceding Isaiah passage. For another, it may have been felt as sacrilegious to sing as Jesus *in propria persona*. And finally, it is in accord with what appears to be Jennens's strategy to allude rather than speak directly. It is the only place in *Messiah* that uses Jesus' own words—and they are thus adjusted. The progression in the three verses is psychologically elegant: 28, the invitation; 29, how I will be affected; and 30, the doctrine, here a mystical Christian paradox.

PART II

20. CHORUS

John 1:29	... Behold, the Lamb of God, that taketh away the sin of the world! ...

Part II opens with the *Agnus dei*, the Lamb of God passage from John, to announce the Passion. It is not strictly Anglican liturgy, although permissible in an alternate Communion Service,[25] but of course it is famous as part of the ancient Roman Catholic mass, and Jennens as Nonjuror is sympathetic to the old forms. In itself it is a reference to Isaiah 53:7 "he is brought as a lamb to the slaughter."

21. ARIA

Isaiah 53:3   He was despised and rejected of men;
a man of sorrows, and acquainted with
grief: . . .

Isaiah 50:6   He gave His back to the smiters, and
His cheeks to them that plucked off the
hair: He hid not His face from shame and
spitting.

22. and 23. CHORUS

Isaiah 53:4   Surely he hath borne our griefs, and
carried our sorrows: . . .

Isaiah 53:5   . . . he was wounded for our transgressions, he was bruised for our iniquities:
the chastisement of our peace was upon
him; and with his stripes we are healed.

24. CHORUS

Isaiah 53:6   All we like sheep have gone astray; we
have turned every one to his own way;
and the Lord hath laid on him the iniquity of us all.

These passages are all from the sections called the "suffering servant"
in Isaiah, taken traditionally to refer mystically to Christ, though
dating from the time of the Babylonian Captivity. In 53:3 the tense is
changed from present to past—the Hebrew tenses in the original are
somewhat ambiguous. In 50:6 the first person is put into third, as in
the previous passage from Matthew. Jennens has shortened 53:3 and
53:4, while 53:5 omits only the initial *But*—which would have spoiled
the logic. Jennens's insertion of 50:6 to break the sequence of 53:3 and
4 shows him not afraid to rearrange to heighten the drama. In the
PB, Isaiah 53 supplies the first lesson for Good Friday matins.

25. ACCOMPAGNATO

Psalm 22:7   All they that see him laugh him to scorn:
they shoot out their lips, and shake their
heads, saying,

26. CHORUS

Psalm 22:8   He trusted in God that he would deliver
him: let him deliver him, if he delight in
him.

27. ACCOMPAGNATO

Psalm 69:21   Thy rebuke hath broken his heart; he is
full of heaviness: he looked for some to
have pity on him, but there was no man;
neither found he any to comfort him.

Psalm 22 is said at Good Friday matins, and Psalm 69 at evensong.
Both are individual laments associated by Christian tradition with the
Passion. Psalm 22 is one of the most desolate, beginning "My God,
my God . . . why hast thou forsaken me? . . . All they that see me
laugh me to scorn"—here again Jennens has changed the person
from first to third to refer to Jesus. In 22:8, which is in the voice of
the scorners, the pronouns are left as is. In this verse the PB version
reads "let him deliver him if he will have him," while the KJV reads
"let him deliver him, seeing he delighted in him"; clearly, Jennens
compared, and this time preferred the KJV as having the sharper
sarcasm (and Handel's music accents it to sharpen it still more).
Psalm 69 is also one of those desolate *cris de coeur:* "Save me, O God,
for the waters are come in unto my soul . . . " and it also is adjusted
to refer to the Passion. The verse used, 21, is identical with the PB
version, except again that Jennens has changed the pronouns from
first person to third.[26] Again he eschews the particular and physical,
"when I was thirsty they gave me vinegar to drink" (22:22). These
psalm passages are all ones that the gospel writers themselves very
consciously adapt to the account of Jesus. Jennens's arrangement is
creative and sensitive: 69:21, for instance, follows dramatically and
psychologically on the preceding.

28. ARIA

Lamentations 1:12   . . . Behold, and see if there be any sorrow like unto his sorrow, . . .

29. ACCOMPAGNATO

Isaiah 53:8   . . . he was cut off out of the land of the
living: for the transgression of thy people
was he stricken.

30. ARIA

Psalm 16:10   But thou didst not leave his soul in hell;
nor didst thou suffer thy Holy One to see
corruption.

Lamentations is associated by old tradition with Good Friday; Jennens has omitted the opening of 1:12 *Is it nothing to you, all ye that pass by?*, and, again, changed the pronoun *my* to *his*, and cut off the ending, again simply to highlight the essential. For the height of sorrow it is indeed appropriate to call on the proverbial weeper of the book of Lamentations. The Isaiah passage again excerpts a small part of the "suffering servant" material, changing *my* to *thy*. And Psalm 16:10 comes in with ingenious continuity, a personal statement *For thou wilt not leave my soul in hell; neither wilt thou suffer thine Holy one to see corruption*, being adapted to continue the narrative of Jesus. This is one of Jennens's boldest strokes, changing the tense as well as pronouns to make it into Christian doctrine—which would be, again, quite according to Nonjuror typology. Psalm 16:10, moreover, is quoted verbatim in Acts 2:27, and in part in Acts 13:35. Acts 2 is part of the Easter evensong service.

31. CHORUS

Psalm 24:7   Lift up your heads, O ye gates; and be ye lift up, ye everlasting doors; and the King of glory shall come in.

Psalm 24:8   Who is this King of glory? The Lord strong and mighty, the Lord mighty in battle.

Psalm 24:9   Lift up your heads, O ye gates; and be ye lift up, ye everlasting doors; and the King of glory shall come in.

Psalm 24:10   Who is this King of glory? The Lord of hosts, he is the King of glory.

This triumphant psalm is the one allotted in the PB to the Ascension Day service, and Jennens has left it as is, eminently singable and dramatic for alternating choral voices. It is the PB version, which differs from the KJV only in *be ye lift up* for *even lift them up*.

32. RECITATIVE

Hebrews 1:5   . . . unto which of the angels said he at any time, Thou art my Son, this day have I begotten thee? . . .

33. CHORUS

Hebrews 1:6   . . . let all the angels of God worship
                                       him.

The rhetoric of exultation continues in these radically shortened
verses from Hebrews. They are from the Epistle reading in the PB for
Christmas.

34. ARIA

Psalm 68:18   Thou art gone up on high, thou hast led
                                       captivity captive: and received gifts for
                                       men; yea, even for thine enemies, that the
                                       Lord God might dwell among them.

35. CHORUS

Psalm 68:11   The Lord gave the word: great was the
                                       company of the preachers.

Psalm 68 is read at Whitsunday matins. In the original it is obscure
and difficult, Dahood tells us;[27] and 68:18 refers, he says, to the
ascent of God on Mount Sinai, while 68:11 refers to *rain* rather than
preaching. But Jennens takes these verses as they are in the PB and
applies them ingeniously to further his spiritual narrative: The Savior
ascends, the Word is given, the Apostles go forth.

36. ARIA

Romans 10:15   . . . How beautiful are the feet of them
                                       that preach the gospel of peace, and bring
                                       glad tidings of good things!

37. CHORUS

Romans 10:18   . . . their sound is gone out unto all
                                       lands, and their words unto the ends of
                                       the world.

As Cuming notes, in these two verses from Romans, Paul quotes,
first, Isaiah 52:7, and then Psalm 19:4. In Romans 10:18 the KJV
translators have Paul quoting something close to the KJV psalm version, logically enough, but Jennens reverts again to the PB version.
KJV reads: *Their line is gone out through all the earth, and their words to*

the end of the world. Sound certainly makes better sense than *line,* especially as we hear the resonant sound itself.

	38. ARIA
Psalm 2:1	Why do the nations so furiously rage together, . . . why do the people imagine a vain thing?
Psalm 2:2	The kings of the earth rise up, and the rulers take counsel together, against the Lord, and against his anointed, . . .
	39. CHORUS
Psalm 2:3	Let us break their bonds asunder, and cast away their yokes from us.
	40. RECITATIVE
Psalm 2:4	He that dwelleth in heaven shall laugh them to scorn: the Lord shall have them in derision.
	41. ARIA
Psalm 2:9	Thou shalt break them with a rod of iron; thou shalt dash them in pieces like a potter's vessel.

With admirable poetic logic Jennens now turns to Psalm 2, as though to say: since the message has been so clear, why does such misery go on here on earth? Here he sticks close to the PB version except for some very interesting changes: in 1, 2, and 3, where the PB (and KJV also) has *heathen,* Jennens puts *nations;* where the PB has *stand up* (and the KJV has *set themselves against*) Jennens puts *rise up;* and where the PB (and KJV) have *cords,* Jennens puts *yokes.* These particular changes suggest another politico-theological link: all Jennens's words here are in the Douay version, the standard English Bible used by English Roman Catholics, and the Nonjurors had Roman sympathies.[28] Each change at the same time makes for a more effective text. The *heathen* are remote, and in our ears the term suggests racism, but the *nations* are political entities we know, then in Jennens's time as in ours. And no one can hear the passage without a sense of its deplorable and poignant timeliness. *Rise up* is unquestionably more vivid than *stand up,* and *yokes* resonates significantly with the preceding "His yoke is easy." But then verse 9 is straight from the KJV, which is more dramatic here than the PB's *Thou shalt bruise them with a rod of iron: and break them in pieces like a potter's vessel.* Clearly, Jennens compared, and chose the more effective: *dash in pieces* is superb.

42. CHORUS

Revelation 19:6	Hallelujah: for the Lord God omnipotent reigneth.
Revelation 11:15	. . . The kingdom of this world is become the kingdom of our Lord, and of his Christ; and he shall reign for ever and ever.
Revelation 19:16	. . . King of Kings, and Lord of Lords.

And then—this was surely a brilliant and original arrangement—he turns to the mystical book of Revelation and distills these visionary passages. Where the KJV has *kingdoms of this world*, Jennens puts *kingdom*, resorting again to the Roman Catholic version, showing both his Nonjuror sympathy and his artistic sense: *kingdoms* suggests political entities, while *kingdom of this world* suggests rather the dispensation of our worldly fallen nature. Handel matches Jennens's boldness with one of his boldest dramatic strokes: the metaphysical moment which as it were validates all the trumpet and drum celebrations, when *this* world is transfigured.

PART III

43. ARIA

Job 19:25	. . . I know that my redeemer liveth, and that he shall stand at the latter day upon the earth:
Job 19:26	And though . . . worms destroy this body, yet in my flesh shall I see God.

And now part III begins with the famous lines from Job. It exemplifies a Christian typology that can no longer be accepted even in seminaries, for *redeemer* is hardly an accurate translation of Hebrew *gô'el*, which is closer to *vindicator* or even *umpire* or *witness*.[29] But perhaps we can call the mistranslation a *felix culpa*, a fortunate mistake, for it gives Handel occasion for the beautifully serene statement of Christian faith. The fact that he takes it from the male voice of Job and gives it to the soprano[30] helps to dissociate it from its original context.

I Corinthians 15:20	For now is Christ risen from the dead, . . . the first fruits of them that sleep.
	44. CHORUS
I Corinthians 15:21	. . . since by man came death, by man came also the resurrection of the dead.
I Corinthians 15:22	For as in Adam all die, even so in Christ shall all be made alive.
	45. ACCOMPAGNATO
I Corinthians 15:51	Behold, I tell you a mystery; We shall not all sleep, but we shall all be changed,
I Corinthians 15:52	In a moment, in the twinkling of an eye at the last trumpet:
	46. ARIA
I Corinthians 15:52	. . . the trumpet shall sound, and the dead shall be raised incorruptible, and we shall be changed.
I Corinthians 15:53	For this corruptible must put on incorruption, and this mortal must put on immortality.
	47. RECITATIVE
I Corinthians 15:54	. . . then shall be brought to pass the saying that is written, Death is swallowed up in victory.
	48. DUET
I Corinthians 15:55	O death, where is thy sting? O grave, where is thy victory?
I Corinthians 15:56	The sting of death is sin; and the strength of sin is the law.
	49. CHORUS
I Corinthians 15:57	But thanks be to God, who giveth us the victory through our Lord Jesus Christ.

The magnificent passages from 1 Corinthians 15 are part of the Easter services, and together with the Job passage are part of the Burial Service. Jennens has made very few and slight changes, and the selections are constructed with a fine economy and progression.

50. ARIA

Romans 8:31   . . . If God be for us who can be against us?

Romans 8:33   Who shall lay any thing to the charge of God's elect? It is God that justifieth.

Romans 8:34   Who is he that condemneth? It is Christ that died, yea rather, that is risen again, who is . . . at the right hand of God, who . . . maketh intercession for us.

51. CHORUS

Revelation 5:12   . . . Worthy is the Lamb that was slain and hath redeemed us to God by His blood to receive power, and riches, and wisdom, and strength, and honour, and glory, and blessing.

Revelation 5:13   . . . Blessing, and honour, . . . glory, and power, be unto Him that sitteth upon the throne, and unto the Lamb for ever and ever.

52. AMEN. CHORUS

These concluding verses are not associated with the liturgy and therefore perhaps represent all the more Jennens's own creative power as a liturgist. In our days, the old Anglican Prayer Book is consigned to oblivion, in a move considered to be desperate or even lethal by many of the Church's critics.[31] But *Messiah* itself survives—and prevails, performing much of the function of liturgy, although it is other things as well. Jennens's fine sense of the way liturgy works shows throughout in his use of Cranmer's PB and in his adjustments of it into an encompassing whole of Christian doctrine. And these concluding passages, where he reaches beyond the PB, make a beautiful and seemly fulfillment of the whole. They are psychologically and emotionally right: the Romans verses celebrate the safety and invulnerability of the saved soul, and then the Revelation verses rise into an access of praise and celebration, with those glorious strings of appositives as though to overwhelm all human capacities. And with the beautiful choral Amen the great work—great words and great music—is complete.

To survey the libretto is to realize the preponderance of the book of Isaiah, especially in the most famous parts. Even the CB verses, which are a small portion of the whole, are mostly ones that quote or refer to Isaiah. It is true that Jesus and all the writers of the CB were thoroughly steeped in Isaiah: Jesus consciously applies the messianic predictions to himself, as the gospel writers record. Paul is the great establisher of Christian typological readings of the prophecies, and the author of the book of Revelation reflects a great deal of the poetic imagery of Isaiah. Isaiah is certainly of all books of the HB the one that had the strongest shaping force on Christianity. We have seen how much Jennens follows the PB readings, and this again is to realize how deeply the Anglican tradition leans on Isaiah, and of course for Jennens himself, there was a passionate investment in the Christian mystical predictive reading of Isaiah, contra the Deists. One effect of *Messiah* is to conflate the HB with the CB in the hearers' minds—and oddly enough, this was just what Jennens intended, to insist on the Christian typological reading of Isaiah.

In this text which is not really very long, Jennens manages to encompass the whole of the Christian worldview: Promise, Incarnation, Passion, Resurrection, and the world-to-come.[32] It is not at all like Bach's great passions, which are dramas focused on events, with Jesus speaking in person. We have noted Jennens's manipulation of pronouns, changing the Psalmist's *I* to *He* referring to Jesus, and Jesus' *I* in the Gospel to a third-person *He*. The effect is not so much a contemplation of the central event of Christianity, the Passion, but rather a whole Christian worldview. By presenting the Christian message so obliquely, mostly through the prophetic poetry of Isaiah, he was able to sidestep certain problems of the CB and its literalism. The HB is of course superior as literature to the CB, which is overtly written in an informal colloquial mode with immediate social purpose, and which is therefore ill adapted to epic development, as Milton's *Paradise Regained* and Klopstock's *Messias* demonstrate. The allusive use of the HB, then, sidesteps dogma and at the same time keeps the long and epic perspective of Christianity. But Jennens by no means compromises Christian doctrine; one might say it is the better mediated for the lack of literalism. Handel did not exactly share Jennens's religious views, and yet one imagines that just because of this delicate obliquity, he was able to accept the text and rise to the occasion. And perhaps for the same reasons, audiences did and still do respond to it without doctrinal anxieties.

This preponderance of Isaiah in *Messiah* reminds us that the whole thing is in large part translated Hebrew poetry, from Isaiah as well as the Psalms. The only nonpoetic parts are, first, the passage from Luke (sec. 14–15), which is straight prose narrative, and second, the passage from Corinthians (sec. 43–49), which is basically Greek hypotactic prose as opposed to the parataxis of Hebrew poetry. But Paul occasionally exploits in impassioned moments the Hebraic poetic idiom, as here, where he echoes Hosea 13:14:

> O death, where is thy sting?
> O grave, where is thy victory?

Perhaps the KJV gives Paul more dignity than he has in the informal *koine* of the Greek CB. At any rate, Handel certainly seems to have a deep appreciation for this Hebraic poetry in its sonorous English translation. In his great anthems he had chosen and set many passages from the Psalms.

It would be a project for a musicologist to undertake to discover how often the parallelistic pattern is retained in the music. Take, for instance,

> Unto us a child is born,
> Unto us a son is given. . . .

Here the two statements, reinforcing and amplifying each other, are matched with similar musical variation: the second part contrasts with and complements the first. Altogether, it is remarkable how Hebrew patterns of parallelism have much in common with our traditional Western musical forms and their patterns of repetition; there is even in many psalms and other poems something like tonality—a return at the end to the "key" of the beginning. Biblical scholars call it *enclosure,* or *ring structure.* A particularly clear pattern is seen in the very formal structure of Psalm 24, in section 32. But Isaiah is especially noted for his elaborate and beautiful parallelistic structures, which are remarkable even in the short excerpts in *Messiah.* Here are some, printed to exhibit the parallels:

Every valley shall be exalted	*a*
and every mountain and hill made low	*a*
the crooked straight	*b*
and the rough places plain.	*b*

This one is very obvious, but very effective too. The first pair may be said to concern the vertical, the second the horizontal.

> But who may abide the day of his coming?
> And who shall stand when he appeareth?

These "rhyme" by being both questions, both voiced in fear and trembling; and the second line intensifies the first: *standing* is more challenging than merely *abiding*, and his *appearance* more immediate than the *day of his coming*. (The Bible pairs in the next line the *refiner's fire* with *fuller's soap* which is, as I pointed out, better left out.)

> Arise,
> Shine,
>
> For thy light is come
> And the glory of the Lord is risen upon thee.

The progression in this quatrain is exquisitely precise: first, one stands, then, to give the message, one "shines"; the reason (*For*) is the arrival of light; what light?—the glory of the Lord, compared, through the word *risen*, to the light of the sun. It is clear now that the message, the *shining*, is the reflected light of the Lord. One of the advantages of metaphor is its power to condense, to say much in little, and *Arise, shine* would seem to be the greatest triumph of condensation, and the more magnificent for the parallel patterns of its musical elaboration. Less obviously poetic, in *Messiah* 44 we have Paul's important piece of doctrinal logic:

Since by man came death,	a_1
by man came also the resurrection of the dead	b_1
For as in Adam all die,	a_2
even so in Christ shall all be made alive.	b_2

Here a_1 and b_1 seem obscure; a_2 and b_2 explain, in order, what is meant. In Handel's music, a_1 and a_2 are similar in harmony, texture, rhythm, and dynamics, and so are b_1 and b_2. The music, that is, reinforces the logic, and one can say that this passage is never better understood than when performed. At the same time, to reinforce the logic is to insist on the poetry, the "rhyme" of thought, and the whole text is infinitely enhanced. Another quatrain is one of Isaiah's most beautiful, in section 11:

> The people that walked in darkness a_1
>   have seen a great light, b_1
> and they that dwell in the land of the shadow of death a_2
>   upon them hath the light shined. b_2

Here, a_2 explains who are these people in a_1, and when we find they live in the *shadow of death*, we realize it is we ourselves, all people. The first b gives us the active apprehension of light, the second gives us the passive reception of it, a combination of active and passive common in Hebrew poetry that gives a great completeness to the verse. Like Isaiah, the Psalms are endless resources for the beauty of these semantic patterns, and it is interesting that Jennens for the most part prefers the PB Psalter, which preserves Cranmer's versions of 1549. This would be in accord with the Nonjurors' preference for the old liturgy; but there are many people even now who prefer the old Psalter to the KJV, on literary grounds. At any rate, in setting so much of Isaiah and Psalms, *Messiah* presents some of the greatest poetry in the world in what may be its most distinguished translation, and perhaps one can say of the whole text that it is never better understood than when performed.

In Germany, Johann Gottfried von Herder, the leader of the modern critical appreciation of Hebrew poetry, recognized the genius of Handel and was particularly entranced with *Messiah*. At Herder's suggestion a performance in English was given at Weimar in 1780, which enravished the young Goethe, and Herder himself translated it into German for ensuing performances. He observed that *Messiah* was a "wahre christliche Epopee in Tönen. . . . Und doch ist alles so einfach! und Worte aus der Bibel—ja Gottlob! nur Worte aus der Bibel; keine schön-gereimte Cantate." ("A true Christian epic in sounds. . . . And then it is all so simple! and words out of the Bible—

yes, praise God! only words out of the Bible; no pretty-rhyming can-
tata.")[33] We know what he means by those "pretty-rhyming cantatas." Handel's oratorio *Susanna* (1759), for instance, had an anony-
mous librettist who turned the dramatic prose of the KJV into stilted
and commonplace rhyming verse:

> A flame like mine, so faithful and so pure
> Shall to the length of latest time endure;
> For heav'n-born virtue doth the warmth inspire,
> And smiling angels fan the godlike fire.

This *Susanna* is one of the marvels of Handel's oeuvre,[34] but not
because of its libretto. The Bible text of *Messiah*, however, remains
"simple" and unproblematic.

True, in a sense it was almost all *pre*selected for Jennens in
Cranmer's PB, deservedly admired for its selection and arrangement
of lessons from the HB, Epistle, Gospel, and Psalm. What Jennens
does achieve by his selections from the PB canon is an arrangement
of beautiful logical, psychological, and doctrinal continuity. Throughout, by careful comparison, he chooses the version that is most singable, and most dramatic, occasionally making a bold adjustment but
not so bold as to seem to depart from Sacred Writ. In "using" Handel,
wedding what he considered the most excellent words in the world
to the most excellent music, he can be said to have achieved his aim.

Edward Fitzgerald in the next century had the liveliest appreciation for Handel as well as for the Rubaiyat of Omar Khayyám. Not
only was he learned in Persian, Spanish, and the classics, but he also
was an accomplished pianist, the kind who would play and sing
through orchestral and vocal scores at home, alone or with friends
about his piano. He understood Handel's Englishness. He writes in
a letter:

> I do indeed take a survey of old Handel's Choruses now and
> then; and am just now looking with great delight at Purcell's
> King Arthur, real noble *English* music, much of it; and assuredly
> the prototype of much Handel. It is said Handel would not ad-
> mire Purcell; but I am sure he adapted himself to English ears
> and sympathies by means of taking up Purcell's vein. [And
> again] I play of evenings some of Handel's great choruses which

are the bravest music after all. I am getting to the true John Bull style of music.[35]

The relationship to Purcell, England's other great composer, is insisted on by recent critics. Winton Dean considers Purcell the "precipitating agent" in the development of Handel's English style; Dean and Paul Henry Lang and Christopher Hogwood all note the pervasiveness and persistence of Purcell's influence and point to many specific points of contact. Purcell had the dramatic instinct and the passion that Handel also excels in; Purcell fosters the English choral tradition. And it might be noted that both Purcell and Handel exploit HB material, according to the English taste.[36] Furthermore, Fitzgerald seems to sense Handel's own lack of committed orthodoxy. He says he prefers the operas and cantatas, even to—

> Magnus Handel, even Messiah. He (Handel) was a good old Pagan at heart and (till he had to yield to the fashionable Piety of England) stuck to Operas and Cantatas, such as Acis and Galatea, Milton's Penseroso, Alexander's Feast, etc., where he could revel and plunge and frolic without being tied down to Orthodoxy. And these are (to my mind) his really great works: these, and his Coronation Anthems, where Human Pomp is to be accompanied and illustrated.[37]

Certainly, Handel's great works have been neglected, and only recently are there hopeful starts made to productions of some of his vast and unappreciated range.

I suppose Fitzgerald is right, in a way, to put *Messiah* more in the background; but on the other hand, we do have to allow for Fitzgerald's committed atheism. What is significant is that Fitzgerald senses Handel's religious openness. Certainly the relationship with Jennens reveals that he was a good deal less of the committed Christian than Jennens was. The stories of his religious raptures during composition have not been substantiated. He was a practical man of the theater and responded—like Shakespeare—to the exigencies of show business and changes in taste. Perhaps at last we can say his human sympathy was too broad to be limited by a single religious orthodoxy. He was, moreover, a child of his time in his rationalism. There is a sense in which he can be called a Deist. Significantly, in his late oratorio *Jephtha* he changed his librettist's line from "What God ordains is right" to Pope's famous "Whatever is, is right."[38] He was a member neither of the Lutheran congregation available to him in London nor of any particular Anglican one, and yet he was regular in church attendance. This might have been due to his professional interest in church music, but also the old permissiveness and breadth of the Anglican church would have appealed to him, as English political freedom did. Lang quotes a contemporary:

> He would often speak of it as one of the great felicities of his life that he was settled in a country where no man suffers any molestation or inconvenience on account of his religious principles.[39]

Dean observes that "there was nothing of the mystic in Handel's personality."[40] Compare Bach's intense mystical Christianity to which his church music is always subordinated, always at service. Dean comments that Handel

> gave the heathen races some of the most ravishing music, especially in *Athalia* and *Theodora*. This refusal to make the righteous more sympathetic than the unrighteous, evidence of his dramatic detachment and freedom from sectarian bias, has been a constant stumbling block to those who sought to turn him into a pillar of the moral establishment.[41]

Fitzgerald was not one of these! But I think it can also be said that Handel had a great religious sensibility. Surely his use of biblical texts and the music itself make this abundantly clear. The humane resources of music and literature would seem to have afforded him spiritual sustenance enough, of a kind which Carlyle was to call Natural Supernaturalism. Bernard Shaw said that in *Messiah* "Handel raised the Bible to a power of transcendence capable of making the unbeliever thrill to 'the glory of the Sublime.'"[42] *Messiah* is exceptional in Handel's oeuvre as lending itself to Christian orthodoxy, and yet the great passages of Isaiah and the guarded use of the CB invest it with a sort of openness. Like Isaiah itself, it can be taken as literalist fundamentalist Christianity, or as the apogee of Hebrew culture, or as one of the great life-enhancing myths of all time.

Finally, Winton Dean concludes:

> The greatness of *Messiah*—Handel's only sacred oratorio in the true sense and therefore untypical—derives on one level from its unique fusion of the traditions of Italian opera, English anthem and German Passion, and on another from the coincidence of Handel's personal faith and creative genius to express, more fully than in any other work of art, the deepest aspirations of the Anglican religious spirit.[43]

And let us add the literary factors: the greatness of Isaiah's poetry, the distinction of its translation into English, and the skill and taste of Charles Jennens the librettist, and Handel's own literary sense in this adopted language of his.

Chapter 6

Robert Lowth and Biblical Literary Criticism

I: The Lectures

In English literary studies Robert Lowth is generally taken as a "precursor of the Romantics," in that reductive way by which romanticists humble the literary notables of the eighteenth century. Of course a poet relates to his predecessors: it used to be that he stood on the shoulders of those who had gone before; now he more often carries the burden of the past and suffers from anxiety of influence. (The truth, perhaps, lies somewhere in between.) But it is the unique distinction of eighteenth-century writers to be reduced to precursorship. True that Robert Lowth precurses indeed in several dimensions: his *Lectures on the Sacred Poetry of the Hebrews* (1753/1793) are considered to have established not only the poet-as-prophet idea basic to Blake, but also the European school of "Orientalism"[1] and the value of "primitive" poetry, whether Hebrew, Greek, Welsh, Scottish, Anglo-Saxon, or Germanic; his *Life of William of Wykham* (1758) is considered a landmark in the development of romantic medievalism; and his *Short Introduction to English Grammar* (1762) gives a new legitimacy and dignity to the vernacular and is keyed to what Wordsworth called "the language really used by men."[2] But if we can for a while throw off this Precursor Fallacy, we can see Lowth as himself a flower of the Enlightenment, that great movement which relegated superstition to the realm of the fictive and extended the light of Reason even over religion and scriptures. James Kugel has given us an elaborate and learned account of Lowth's precursors in the matter of biblical criticism, neatly turning the tables on precursorism.[3] But it is Lowth's distinction to have taken up the best of his predecessors' work and set the criticism of scripture fairly in the context of secular literary criticism. He more or less dismisses the phonological analysis of Hebrew verse—by stress patterns or quantity—as too vexed to be serviceable (as indeed many scholars still do), and establishes semantic parallelism as in fact the definitive "metrical" system, and observes that this "meter" is translatable. And his lectures and textual annotations bring into play the whole known world of literature and scholarship and are profoundly suggestive of critical method, not only in this particular area of semantic parallelism, but also for the phenomenology of metaphor.

Lowth was born in 1710 in the cathedral close of Winchester, son of Canon William Lowth; he attended Winchester College and New College, Oxford, took orders, and rose to the bishopric of London. He was offered the Archbishopric of Canterbury, but declined on grounds of ill health in 1783, and died in 1787, Fellow of the Royal Society in London, and also Fellow of the Royal Society of Göttingen. It was in 1741–50 that as Professor of Poetry at Oxford he delivered the *Praelectiones Academicae de Sacra Poesi Hebraeorum*. In 1753 they were published in their original Latin and were widely read, most notably in Germany, where the learned J. D. Michaelis published an edition with his notes in 1775; this expanded revision was translated and published in England in 1793.[4] It consists of thirty-four lectures, ranging through all the Hebrew Bible, with classical analogues and all available scholarship, rabbinical and Christian, lacking only, as Michaelis notes, the Syriac and the Arabic.[5] Lowth's choice of subject was portentous. Oxford, deeply imbued in classical learning, had long kept secular literature compartmentalized from theology and scripture, and now the Professor of Poetry boldly breaches the separating wall. It is somewhat like the case of Milton, long brooding over his possible epic subject, settling at last on the greatest, the divine Christian myth; so Lowth as critic, as Professor of Poetry, takes on the greatest challenge, the greatest because sacred, the poetry of the HB. By addressing the poetry rather than historical prose narrative he can rather conveniently sidestep the theologically contentious issue of the historicity of the Bible.[6] As a clergyman of course he was bound to underwrite the orthodox Anglican position. His patron, Bishop Hoadley, was one of the leaders of the attack on Deists such as Anthony Collins. At the same time, Hoadley is considered a leader in "the demystification of religion," a Latitudinarian who held that the Lord's Supper was purely commemorative. One suspects that Lowth held similar views; there is certainly nothing of the mystic temper in his criticism, and his sermons are said to have been practical and prudential. In the *Lectures,* he stays within a protective cocoon of orthodox hermeneutics: Moses wrote the Pentateuch, the Song of Solomon is allegory, Isaiah predicts Jesus Christ, and so on. But he applies thoroughly secular artistic criteria to the poetry and argues that just because these texts are sacred we owe them all the more the respect of analysis. Recurrently, he claims that the sacred poetry outdoes the Greek and Roman classics and better illustrates the principles of art. Even the Latin of the lectures and his Latin versions of scripture were admired for their elegance. But in our English version we have the advantage of the added notes by Michaelis and others.

While it had been generally accepted that such books as Psalms and Job were "poetical," Lowth makes the new case that the prophets also write as poets and explores the whole matter of what poetry consists in. He cites the two Hebrew words for poem, *mizmor* and *mashal,* and under these two heads might be subsumed his main substance. For *mizmor* means *cut* or *divided,* into—Lowth would say— short and equal sentences, and this expresses the principle of parallelism; and *mashal* means *he likened, he spoke in parables,* and this expresses the characteristic of figurative language (1:69, 77). He grants of course that both parallelism and figures do occur in prose, but only occasionally. He takes note of the "alphabetic" (acrostic) poems— certain Psalms, Prov. 31:10–end, and Lamentations—observing that in them the verses are very regular, with a high degree of parallelism, that is. But where parallelism is occasional in prose, in Hebrew poetry it is *the* distinguishing feature. He refutes the various elaborate efforts to discern classical meter in Hebrew,[7] and pretty well dismisses any attempt to discern sound patterns of any sort as irretrievable, musing on the delicate evanescence of any spoken language now dead: "the vital grace is wanting, the native sweetness is gone . . . " (1:86). He allows that there may be some stress patterns in Hebrew poetry but dismisses any arguments for them as systematic. What is essential to poetry is *numbers,* and Hebrew poetry is indeed metrical in *numbers,* not as Greek or Latin or English, but in sentences in pairs (or occasionally in triplets) running parallel to one another. He speculates that the practice may have originated in performance by alternating choirs: the women "answered" one another in Miriam's song of triumph, and in the song "Saul hath smote his thousands, And David his ten thousands" (2:28–29). He brings Ecclesiasticus to witness the association with music: Jesus ben Sira puts among the famous men to be praised—

> Leaders of the people by their counsels
> and by their knowledge of learning meet for the people,
> wise and eloquent in their instructions,
> Such as found out musical tunes
> and recited verses in writing.
>
> (1:81; Ecclus. 44:4–5)

Moreover, ben Sira seems to describe a kind of binary worldview at the base of the distich pattern:

> Good is set against evil
> and life against death;
> so is the godly against the sinner
> and the sinner against the godly.
> So look upon all the works of the most High,
> and there are two and two, one against the other.
>
> (1:100; Ecclus. 33:14–15)

(Cognitive science at the present time might grant that binarism is a basic psychological process.) And so the Hebrew poet follows suit with his lines, two and two, one against the other.

> The Hebrew poets frequently express a sentiment with the utmost brevity and simplicity, illustrated by no circumstances, adorned with no epithets (which in truth they seldom use); they afterward call in the aid of ornament; they repeat, they vary, they amplify the same sentiment; and adding one or more sentences which run parallel to each other, they express the same or a similar, and often a contrary sentiment, in nearly the same form of words. . . . These forms again are diversified by notes of admiration, comparison, negation, and more particularly interrogation, whence a singular degree of force and elevation is frequently added to the composition. (1:100)

It would be hard to fault this description. He illustrates throughout with apt quotations, often in his own translation, varying somewhat from the KJV, and generally printed according to the parallelism. Further—and this is a very important point—Lowth observes that accurate translation "from the Hebrew into the prose of any other language, whilst the same form of the sentences remain, will still retain, even as far as relates to versification, much of its native dignity . . . " (1:71). As Roston remarks, "Lowth's theory of translation was . . . implicit in his exposition of parallelism";[8] for if the poetic quality depends upon balance of ideas and phrases, the translation must keep as literal as possible. If it is translated into *verse*, the pattern is lost. Lowth adduces the Renaissance Hebrew scholar, Azariah dei Rossi, the greatest of the Precursors, who said: "Is it not evident, that if you translate [Hebrew poems] into another language, they still retain this metrical form, if not perfect, at least in a great degree? which cannot possibly take place in those poems the metre of which consists in the number and quantity of syllables" (1:72). Those who are not Hebraists must make this point with trepidation. Sometimes it seems that one is in Plato's cave seeing the multiform shadow variations of a Psalm, say, in the four or five languages one knows, and even in ten or so different *English* versions, while the Hebrew version is up there in the mind of God. But on the other hand if Azariah dei Rossi himself considers the form outstandingly translatable because of the parallelism, surely we can take the courage to say so also. Lowth did say so with impunity.

Lowth on parallelism is fairly well known; Lowth on figurative language is not so well known and is a mine of critical sense. First, he makes a delightful declaration which should endear him to all students: he will clear the ground of all those Greek terms for subtly differentiated figures of speech, devised by rhetoricians for Greek and Latin literature, and will use a simple classification: *metaphor,* and its extension, *allegory;* the *simile* or *comparison;* and *prosopopaeia* or *personification*. First, he describes our field, our data:

> The whole course of nature, this immense universe of things, offers itself to human contemplation, and affords an infinite variety, a confused assemblage, a wilderness, as it were, of images. . . . (1:116)

(The terms anticipate William James's vision of the "blooming, buzz-
ing confusion" of sensory data.) Lowth goes on to say that of all these
data,

> The least clear and evident are those which are explored by rea-
> son and argument; the more evident and distinct are those which
> are formed from the impressions made by external objects on the
> senses; and of these, the clearest and most vivid are those which
> are perceived by the eye. Hence poetry abounds most in those
> images which are furnished by the senses, and chiefly those of
> the sight; in order to depict the obscure by the more manifest,
> the subtile by the more substantial; and as far as simplicity is its
> object, it pursues those ideas which are most familiar and most
> evident. . . . (1:117–18)

Poetic imagery can be derived—he classifies now—from (1) objects
from nature, (2) objects from common life, (3) things sacred, and (4)
history. He proceeds with beautiful and widely spread biblical examples. Light and darkness are frequent:

> No longer shall thou have the sun for thy light by day,
> Nor by night shall the brightness of the moon enlighten thee:
> For Jehovah shall be to thee an everlasting light
> And thy God shall be thy glory.
>
> (1:129–30; Isa. 60:19)

Water and drought, weather and farming, desert and mountain are
recurrent. The two particular mountains, Lebanon—tall, cedar-cov-
ered, and majestic—and Carmel—rich and fruitful—are wonderfully
used, he says, in the Song of Solomon to represent the male and the
female. "It is the first duty of a critic," he argues, "to remark, as far
as possible, the situation and habits of the author, the natural history of his country, and the scene of the poem" (1:139). Accordingly
he explains such processes as the threshing and winnowing of
grain.

> Jehovah threshes out the heathen as corn, tramples them under
> his feet, and disperses them. He delivers the nations to Israel to
> be beaten in pieces by an indented flail, or to be crushed by their

brazen hoofs. He scatters his enemies like chaff upon the mountains, and disperses them with the whirlwind of his indignation. (1:148)

(He gives referents for all these, in Habakkuk, Joel, Jeremiah, Isaiah, Micah, and the Psalms.) He notes how Homer also in a famous passage uses the figure of threshing for a victorious army treading down the enemy, but even Homer, he says, "still falls greatly short of the Hebrew boldness and sublimity" (1:151). The powerful image of the winepress for God's vengeance is unique to the Hebrews, he thinks, and he quotes from Isaiah 63 the famous passage on the grapes of wrath. He implies that the very commonness of the imagery is what keeps those texts accessible. In a glorious insight he quotes the vengeful Jehovah:

I will wipe Jerusalem
As a man wipeth a dish:
He wipeth it, and turneth it upside down.
(1:154; 2 Kings 21:13)

"The meanness of the image is fully equalled by the plainness and inelegance of the expression; and yet such is its consistency, such the propriety of its application, that I do not scruple to pronounce it sublime" (1:155). Bravo, Robert Lowth! Out of all the poetic diction and elaborate periphrases that seem to us to vitiate much eighteenth-century poetry comes this bold, plain piece of literary criticism. Let us not scruple to call it a historic moment.

Further, he sets out the metaphor project for critics: "The mind should . . . exert itself to discover, if possible, the connexion between the literal and figurative meanings . . . " (1:155). And he proceeds to categorize biblical figures and comment on a wealth of examples. Metaphors from sacred topics may include ritual; indeed, "The whole system of the Hebrew rites is one great and complicated allegory . . . " (1:170), and he relates Psalm 104 to temple usages.[9] Of images drawn from history the Hebrew poets had a great store, simply because they *had* a great deal of history, and it was a religious duty to know the destruction of Sodom and Gomorrah, the Exodus, the Law on Mount Sinai, and so on. Under the rubric of *allegory,* Lowth broaches the matter of typology, which of course is not of much interest to secular criticism; certainly Lowth endorsed the orthodox Christian reading of the Hebrew scriptures, which will now, to the literary critic, seem forced. But under *personification*, he makes an eloquent display: the strange richness of the figure of Wisdom in Proverbs 8:

> When he prepared the heavens I was present . . . ,
> When he planned the foundations of the earth
>   Then was I by him as his offspring;

the sweetness of Psalm 85:

> Mercy and Truth are met together
> Righteousness and Peace have kissed each other;

the "tremendous image in Isaiah [5:14], of Hades extending her throat and opening her insatiable and immeasurable jaws"; the way nations and peoples are personified, like "the virgin daughter of Babylon"; the animation of nature—and he gathers a little anthology of these:

> Let the Heavens rejoice, and let the Earth be glad;
> And let them proclaim through the nations, Jehovah reigneth.
>   (1 Chron. 16:31)
> Let the Sea roar, and all that it containeth
> The World, and the inhabitants thereof:
> Let the Floods clap their hands;
> Let the Mountains break forth into harmony;
>   (Ps. 98:7–8)
> Before Jehovah, for he cometh,
> For he cometh to judge the earth;
>   (Ps. 96:13)
> The Waters saw thee, O God!
> The Waters saw thee, they were grievously troubled;
>   (Ps. 77:6)
> The Deep uttered his voice;
> And lifted up his hands on high;
>   (Hab. 3:10)

and perhaps the greatest personification of all in the Voice of the
Whirlwind:

Canst thou send forth the Lightnings,
    and will they go?
Shall they say unto thee,
    Behold here we are?

(Job 38:35)

He cites also the extravagances of the God-figures, such as "the
sword of Jehovah" (Jer. 47:6). And there is the kind of personification
which ascribes a probable speech to a real person, as in the "inimita-
ble ode of the prophetess Deborah," where the mother of Sisera
imagines with her women the reasons for the delay of Sisera's return,
when we know he lies dead by the hand of Jael (1:289–94). It is Isaiah,
however, that Lowth acclaims above all others as "the sublimest of
poets," and he presents Isa. 14:4–27 as exhibiting almost every form
of prosopopaeia.

In lectures 14, 15, and 16, Lowth expatiates on that great eighteenth-century concern, "the Sublime," which may seem somewhat
tiresome to us now. We might, though, think of it as the way that
aestheticians tried to cope with experience that seemed to transcend
the rational. At any rate it gives Lowth occasion for good comment—
on Job, for instance. By exhibiting the difference between the clearly
prose framework and the clearly poetic body, he further elucidates
the idea of Hebrew poetry, "the distribution of the sentences in parallel patterns of marked regularity," and the diction as "plain, correct,
chaste, and temperate," and yet the passionate feeling even as in
Job's first outburst:

Let the day perish, I was born in it,
And the night [which] said a man is conceived.

(1:310–14)

Another exhibit contrasting prose and verse he draws from the last
books of Deuteronomy. Chapters 28 to 31 give Moses' oration to the
people of Israel, and even "with all its vehemence and impetuosity"

the idiom is nevertheless ordinary. But the "Song of Moses," chapter 32, "on the contrary, consists of sentences, pointed, energetic, concise, and splendid; . . . the sentiments are truly elevated and sublime, the language bright and animated, the phraseology uncommon . . . " (1:325). (Chap. 32 is generally considered by scholars now to be late, about 700 BCE, or contemporary with the great prophets, and in their idiom.)

Finally, there is the problem of Inspiration, and here Lowth treads warily. He endeavors, he says, to detract nothing from "that inspiration which proceeds from higher causes," but is of the opinion "that the Divine Spirit by no means takes such an entire possession of the mind of the Prophet, as to subdue or extinguish the character and genius of the man . . . ," and in the writings of Moses or David or Isaiah we may observe their respective characteristics. They have excelled all others in "the sublime"—for the greatness and sublimity of the subject itself, and "the splendour and magnificence of the imagery" (2:347). He cites Genesis

> And God said, Let there be light
> and there was light;

and the Psalm

> For he spoke, and it was;
> He commanded, and it stood fast;

(Ps. 33:9)

and Job and the moment of creation

> When the morning stars sang together
> And all the sons of God shouted for joy.

And there is the description "carried on by a kind of continued negation" in Job and Psalm 139, when the sublimities of nature are found to be inferior and inadequate to the mind of God.

> If I take the wings of the morning
> And dwell in the extreme parts of the ocean;
> There also thy hand shall lead me,
> And thy right hand shall hold me.

"Here we find the idea of Infinity perfectly expressed, though it be perhaps the most difficult of ideas to impress upon the mind . . . " (2:355–56). Such analysis as this led Samuel Holt Monk to declare that Lowth anticipates Burke and Kant "in his explanation of what occurs when the imagination strives to grasp a reality beyond the possibility of literal description."[10] Interrogation, Lowth notes, occurs frequently and is "admirably calculated to impress the mind with a very forcible idea of the Divine power."

> For Jehovah God of Hosts hath decreed;
>   and who shall disannul it?
> And it is his hand that is stretched out;
>   and who shall turn it back?
>
> (1:347–58; Isa. 14:26–27)

Further, in the *Lectures*, he takes the Hebrew word *nabi* to mean prophet, poet, and musician, all three, and does not except two women, Miriam and Deborah. He notes that the books of Daniel and Jonah, both late, are not poetry like all the other prophets and explains that indeed Hebrew poetry suffered a decline after the Babylonian captivity. He characterizes each poetic prophet's style, always giving first place to Isaiah. Greek and Roman "prophecy" is rare, he observes, and while we have very few of their oracles, what we do have suggests that "they were not upon the best terms with the Muses" (2:101–2); but then Virgil's Fourth Eclogue is the exception, and Lowth accepts the tradition that it is genuine Christian prophecy. He classifies biblical poetry according to genres: elegy, proverb, odes of various kinds. As for drama, he considers that the Song of Solomon does not fall into this class (though Milton whom he does not mention had seen it so), and Job, though comparable to *Oedipus Rex* and *Oedipus Coloneus*, is not a drama either. He notes the importance of the prose framework, and the beauty and perfection of the whole, the "poetic conformation" being extremely regular and correct. In all, it "claims first place in Hebrew poetry." At the end of the last lecture he urges his hearers to go on with the study of Hebrew, as "deserving the attention of every liberal mind" (2:434).

II: Lowth's Isaiah

As Professor of Poetry at Oxford, Lowth delivered the *Praelectiones* in 1741–50, and they were published in 1753, a triumph of the printer's art for the newly founded Clarendon Press, with a Latin text, quotations in Hebrew, Greek, and Latin, and copious notes.[11] As bishop of London, years later, he brought out his own version of Isaiah in English, with a *Preliminary Dissertation* and extensive polyglot notes, 1778, in two volumes.[12] It is in no way at odds with the earlier work. It refers at times to the *Praelectiones* for corroboration and restates the principles of parallelism even more succinctly, explaining the "Rhythmus of things," "rhythm of propositions," and "harmony of sentences." In a useful new book *Critics of the Bible 1724–1873*, John Drury has included selections from Lowth's famous *Lectures* and placed them in context. However, for the poetics, Drury might have done better to extract from the less famous *Preliminary Dissertation* to Isaiah, for it is more considered than the *Lectures* and has the elegance of Lowth's own English rather than Gregory's translation of Lowth's elegant Latin. In a note, Drury quotes from the *Preliminary Dissertation* the focal definition:

> the correspondence of one Verse, or Line, with another, I call Parallelism. When a Proposition is delivered, and a second is subjoined to it, or drawn under it, equivalent, or contrasted with it in Sense; or similar to it in the form of Grammatical Construction; these I call Parallel Lines; and the words, or phrases, answering one to another in the corresponding Lines, Parallel Terms.[13]

Lowth declares that a knowledge of the system of parallelism is essential to emendation as well as to interpretation, and he gives various examples, such as Isaiah 28:15:

> We have made a covenant with death
> and with the grave we have made——

What? asks Lowth. It *must* be agreement or bargain or treaty, although the Hebrew word does not mean this elsewhere. Vitringa, the best preceding commentator, concurs that it must be *transactionem*

(KJV has "with hell are we at *agreement*," Lowth puts *treaty*, NEB has *pact*). He declares:

> It could not otherwise have been known that the word has this meaning; it is the Parallelism alone, that determines it to this meaning. (1:39)

He anticipates hereby Renan's *"sens conseillée par le parallelisme"* and Gevirtz's "To be indifferent to the art is to risk indifference to the meaning."[14]

There is an advantage, Lowth claims, in translating the Hebrew into English. Where Tyndale had declared English is by nature a "thousand times" closer to Hebrew than Latin or Greek,[15] Lowth argues that English itself has been modified by close verbal translation from Hebrew and has, as it were, become more like it. The Bible "has by degrees molded our language into such conformity with that of the original Scriptures, that it can upon occasion assume the Hebrew character without appearing altogether forced and unnatural" (1:52). He declares it the business of the translator to be as close as possible to his original; for whatever the interpretation is, "Spiritual, Mystical, Allegorical, Analogical, or the like, they must all intirely depend upon the Literal sense" (1:52). For instance, Isaiah 51:20 in the Septuagint has the Greek for "like parboiled beet," but it should in fact be "like an oryx in the toils" (the KJV has "as a wild bull in a net"); and Lowth gleefully quotes Theodoret's misguided exegesis of the parboiled beet! Accuracy matters. Furthermore, the translator must work from the best text, and he surveys all those available, anticipating the forthcoming Variorum Hebrew edition of Kennicott. He refers with pleasant irony to superstitious tradition such as the Hebrew faith that all copyists were inspired by God to be accurate, and the Roman Catholic tradition that takes the Vulgate as God's authentic version. In fact, he points out, the Almighty God has permitted innumerable variants in the six hundred or so extant copies— which might give the exegete pause. But he observes that Aristotle's *Poetics* is also a very corrupt text, and it is still "the Great Code of Criticism" (1:60).[16]

He reiterates his policy of using on the Bible the same scholarly methods that one would use for Greek and Latin authors. The translator must confess the difficulties and lay them before the reader.

He surveys the case of Isaiah (still well known to be full of textual problems) and lists the most reliable texts. The Septuagint, for instance, is very useful in this case, for the "Seventy" used a Hebrew text older than any we have. The Masoretes he consistently objects to, because their version is very late and remote from the originals, and the vowel pointing they did often represent a misreading. Moreover, they had lost the understanding of parallelism which so often elucidates the sense.

He concludes the *Preliminary Dissertation* with a comment on the KJV:

> I have ventured to call this a New Translation, though much of our Vulgar Translation is retained in it. As the Style of that translation is not only excellent in itself, but has taken possession of our ear, and of our taste, to have endeavoured to vary from it, with no other design than that of giving something new instead of it, would have been to disgust the reader, and to represent the Sense of the Prophet in a more unfavourable manner. . . . As to the style and language [the KJV] admits of no improvement; but in respect of the sense and the accuracy of interpretation, the improvements of which it is capable are great and numberless. (1:72–73)

These are unexceptionable principles, surely. Frequently our modern translations do seem to go in for merest novelty and are accordingly, as Lowth would say, disgusting.

Lowth's Isaiah is in two volumes, volume 1 comprising the *Preliminary Dissertation*, 74 pages, and the text itself, which takes up 174. Volume 2 consists solely of notes and takes up 283 pages, a fatter volume than the first, and full of interest and insight. In the notes, he gives first a few pages of historical overview, understanding the whole book to have been written by the Isaiah whose career we know, Isaiah of Jerusalem, or Isaiah I, fl. 740–700 BCE. (Now, everyone grants that chaps. 40–66 are written later, ca. 537–520 BCE, by an unknown referred to as Isaiah II, or the Deutero-Isaiah; and some hold by yet a third author, Trito-Isaiah, of chaps. 56–66.) He prints the lines throughout according to the parallel patterns, reverting to prose paragraphs for the narrative passages that are clearly not poetic, such as 36–38, just as our new versions do now. Lowth was presumably the first to do this. On occasion he indicates speakers, as for 63:1–6, Chorus and Messenger. (The NEB uses quotation marks here to indicate different voices.) He does not follow the KJV practice of italicizing elements interpolated for clarity; this probably suggests that Lowth felt he was not interpolating anything at all. Throughout he puts *Jehovah* for the KJV's *Lord*, which certainly suggests the Hebrew. But then he puts *Hades* for hell (5:14) which certainly suggests kinship with the classics. However, Hebrew *sheol* *is* more like Greek Hades than Christian hell. He determinedly applies secular literary critical method, supplying analogues from Homer, Theocritus, Virgil, Ovid, Lucretius, Horace, and modern writers; and often after Homer's Greek he supplies Pope's translation into English. He also refers in a literary-critical way to a wonderfully broad range of the Bible itself: historical books, Psalms, other prophets, Job and other Wisdom Literature, and the Apocrypha too.

The notes refer also to a very wide range of scholarship. He quotes Hebrew, Greek, and Latin, and refers to a multitude of manuscripts. For Arabic, he applies to an Oxford Arabist, Dr. Hunt, and refers to George Sale, the learned translator of the Koran (1734). He refers to his father William Lowth's *Commentary on the Prophets* (1714–25), to Newton on the prophecies, to Grotius, to Vitringa. He uses historians' and travelers' accounts, copiously, on the principle that to understand a text, you must understand the civilization from which it emerged. He corrects the notorious mistake, "The voice of him that crieth in the wilderness," so misunderstood by all four gospel writers, to "A voice crieth: In the wilderness prepare ye the way of Jehovah" (40:3), which restores the parallelism (*in the wilderness* matches *in the desert* in the next line); and he explains in a note how Eastern monarchs sent harbingers before them to prepare the way. The Romans called them *stratores*. To explain "Every valley shall be exalted, and the mountains and hills made plain" (40:4), he quotes Diodorus Siculus's account of Semiramis's marches into Media and Persia:

> She ordered the precipices to be digged down and the hollows to be filled up; at great expense she made a shorter and more expeditious road, which to this day is called from her the road of Semiramis. (2:192 [Lowth's translation])

The metaphorical reading of this Isaiah passage seems sufficient, but nevertheless it is interesting to know that on occasion the engineering was literally performed. How just is Lowth's declaration that *all* interpretations depend upon the correct literal translation! Occasionally he takes up a comparative-religion attitude: for 28:26, where God is praised for the crops, he observes that all nations have attributed the science of agriculture to their deities and quotes Ecclesiasticus, the Roman Lucretius, and the Greek Aratus to that effect, and proceeds to describe the threshing process referred to in the next verses, citing four authorities (2:152).

Throughout the notes one has a vivid sense of the personality of Lowth, especially when he indulges himself in little touches of almost Humean irony. On Isaiah's recommending—sensibly—a poultice of figs to cure what was apparently King Hezekiah's case of blood poisoning (38:21) he comments: "God in effecting this miraculous cure was pleased to order the use of means not improper for that end," and quotes Pliny on the medical aspect (2:182). Again, where Vitringa feared to emend his Hebrew text, Lowth comments: "They that hold the present Hebrew text to be absolutely infallible, must make their way through it as best they can: but they ought surely to give us somewhat that has at least the appearance of sense"—which he proceeds to gather from a comparison with the Chaldee, the usual text being both "corrupted and defective." Certainly Lowth is a bold emendator. Matthew Arnold considered that he "was rash and took liberties."[17] Arnold owned what was the most up-to-date commentary on Isaiah, that of Gesenius,[18] the great German author of the Hebrew Lexicon and Hebrew Grammar, but in fact Arnold often follows Lowth's emendations in his own version. A modern scholar has great praise for Lowth's scholarship. He observes that Gesenius was much influenced by Lowth, and "where he disagrees with Lowth he is generally wrong."[19]

In his appreciation of the brilliance of Hebrew metaphor, Lowth is perhaps at his most characteristic best. In a place where the KJV is somewhat obscure:

And the inhabitant shall not say, I am sick:
The people that dwell therein *shall be* forgiven *their* iniquity,
(33:24)

Lowth illuminates by citing the analogous passage from the Psalms:

> Who forgiveth all thy sin;
> And healeth all thine iniquities.
>
> (Ps. 103:3)

In each case the two lines explain each other by their parallelism. Lowth adds, "And our blessed Saviour reasons with the Jews on the same principle: 'Whether it is easier to say to the sick of the palsy, thy sins are forgiven thee; or to say, Arise, and take up thy bed and walk'" (Mark 2:9). In fact the CB sometimes shows consciousness of the Hebrew parallelistic tradition, and sometimes not. It would seem from this that Jesus knew it well, if the gospel writers did not always. This whole note exemplifies Lowth's alert analogizing and success in using literary criticism for exegesis. He acclaims the vivid anti-idol passage in 44:12ff. as surpassing all others on the common theme and refers cheerfully to no other than Horace wittily mocking the god Priapus made out of the trunk of a fig tree (2:206). In another passage on idols, where the KJV following Tyndale has "thou shalt cast them away as a menstruous cloth" (which I understand to be justified in the Hebrew),[20] Lowth silently changes to "Thou shalt cast them away like a polluted garment" (30:22) but comments only on how it is the same prohibition that Moses makes in Deut. 7:25, which speaks of "abomination."

In the vivid put-down of women's vanities in Isaiah 3 Lowth changes the wonderful Jacobean ideas of Eastern accoutrements to ones that result from his researches into Oriental customs. The KJV lists:

> *Their* tinkling ornaments *about their feet,* and *their* cauls, and *their* round tires like the moon, the chains, and the bracelets, and the mufflers, the bonnets, and the ornaments of the legs, and the headbands, and the tablets, and the earrings, the rings, and nose jewels, the changeable suits of apparel, and the mantles, and the wimples, and the crisping pins, the glasses, and the fine linen, and the hoods, and the vails [sic].

Lowth revises to:

the ornaments of the feet-rings, and the net-works, and the cres-
cents; the pendents [sic], and the bracelets, and the thin vails;
the tires, and the fetters, and the zones; and the perfume-boxes,
and the amulets, the rings, and the jewels of the nostril, the
embroidered robes, and the tunics; and the cloaks, and the little
purses, the transparent garments, and the fine linen vests, and
the turbans and the mantles. (3:18–24)

The list shows a conscientious effort on the part of the bishop to cope
with those difficult matters, and the notes delightfully refer to
learned commentary: a traveler Pietro della Valle who had married
an Assyrian lady and consequently well knew a *network* from a *zone*,
as well as Xenophon, Sandys, Pliny, Shaw, Ezekiel, Russell, Clemens
Alexandrinas Julius Pollux, Aristophanes, and lastly Shroederus of
Marburg who had published a treatise on this very passage, a "Com-
mentarius Philologico-Criticus De Vestitu Mulierum Hebraearum" in
1745. (It is amusing to see the variations in subsequent translations
of Isaiah, and to see how other cultures deal with these clothes. The
Jerusalem Bible both in French and English includes *mantillas*, the
NEB includes *lockets* and *flounced skirts*, RSV has *handbags*. It may be
that every generation must have its new translation.)

It is perhaps a little surprising that Lowth with all his appreciation of the bold plainness of Hebrew style sometimes himself changes
the simple KJV into ornate latinisms. In 47:6 where the KJV read

Upon the ancient hast thou very heavily laid thy yoke,

Lowth has

Even upon the aged didst thou greatly aggravate the weight of
thy yoke.

(Here the Anchor seems to be the winner: "On the aged you made
your yoke very heavy.")[21] Perhaps most unfortunate are his changes
in 60: the KJV is

Arise, shine, for thy light is come
And the glory of the Lord is risen upon thee.
For, behold, the darkness shall cover the earth

and gross darkness the people:
but the Lord shall arise upon thee
and his glory shall be seen upon thee
And the Gentiles shall come to thy light
and Kings to the brightness of thy rising.

(60:1–3)

Lowth:

Arise, be thou enlightened; for thy light is come;
And the glory of Jehovah is risen upon thee.
For behold, darkness shall cover the earth;
And a thick vapour the nations:
But upon thee shall Jehovah arise;
And his glory upon thee shall be conspicuous.
And the nations shall walk in thy light;
And kings in the brightness of thy sun-rising.

Here, the Anchor as representative of best contemporary scholarship would seem to bear out the KJV rather than Lowth, and Lowth's latinate words surely deflect the splendor of the KJV. "Be thou enlightened" and "shall be conspicuous" are utter disasters.

Generally, Lowth's biblical criticism neglects theology, but in dealing with Isaiah, theology can hardly be sidestepped, specifically in the passages considered by orthodox Christianity to predict the advent, career, and sacrifice of Christ. Lowth's strategies here are interesting. On "Behold, a virgin shall conceive, and bear a son, and shall call his name Immanuel" (7:14), he appends a full discussion of learned opinion and adds what he understands to be "the obvious and literal meaning of the prophecy":

within the time that a young woman, now a virgin, should conceive and bring forth a child, and that child should arrive at such an age as to distinguish between good and evil, that is, within a few years, (compare ch. VIII.4) the enemies of Judah should be destroyed. (2:64)

But, he goes on to say, the manner of the prophecy is so portentous that "in minds prepared by the general expectation of a great Deliverer to spring from the house of David" it was bound to take on more meaning. Even Micah, Isaiah's contemporary, he says, appears to understand it as prophesying Messiah (5:3). Lowth goes on:

> St. Matthew therefore in applying this prophecy to the birth of Christ, does it not merely in the way of accommodating the words of the Prophet to a suitable case not in the Prophet's view; but takes it in its strictest, clearest, and most important sense, and applies it according to the original design and principal intention of the Prophet. (2:65)

Thus is orthodoxy preserved. Lowth's understanding in all these cases of what is called typology, the interpretation of the HB in terms of the CB, is double: a literal historical reading plus a symbolic predictive Christian reading. "It is almost the constant practice of the Prophet to connect in like manner deliverances temporal with spiritual. . . . And thus the chapters from XL to XLIX, inclusive, plainly relating to the deliverance from the Captivity of Babylon, do in some parts as plainly relate to the greater deliverance by Christ" (2:67–68). On 26:19, "Thy dead men shall live," he explains that "Resurrection of the dead was at that time a popular and common doctrine: for an image which is assumed in order to express or represent another in the way of allegory or metaphor, whether poetical or prophetical, must be an image commonly known and understood" (2:144); this appears to limit the image here to the metaphorical and not to imply literal resurrection.

Starting at chapter 40, he is obliged to address the subject of the Return. Here, he says, "the Evangelical sense of the Prophecy is so apparent . . . that some interpreters cannot see that it has any other" (2:184), but he insists on the historical sense. "I have not the least doubt that the Return of the Jews from the captivity of Babylon is the first, though not the principal, thing in the Prophet's view" (2:186). He elucidates the historical sense amply, describing Cyrus and his strategy of destroying the control of the Euphrates effected by Nebuchadnezzar and so causing flooding which led to the capture of Babylon (2:207–8).[22] But there is no question that Lowth supports the Christian typological interpretation in general and throughout. In those passages called "the suffering servant" (in chaps. 42, 50, 52, 53)—"Surely he hath borne our griefs," etc.—he unquestionably applies the material to Jesus, and yet at the same time manages to remind us that Jesus and the gospel writers were themselves making the application. He says that it is Matthew who has applied the words "Behold my servant" (42:1) directly to Christ (2:197), for example. And on 61:1 "he hath sent one to proclaim liberty to the captives" he notes that it is Jesus who applies the text to himself, Luke 4:18–19. These are suggestions that somehow leave open the rational understanding of the connections between Isaiah and the Gospels.

This whole edition of Isaiah is clearly a labor of love. Lowth had long ago declared his high evaluation of Isaiah's poetry; he had done a translation into Latin of what he calls the "great ode" that is chapter 14:4–27, starting "How hath the oppressor ceased! the golden city ceased!" and including "How art thou fallen from heaven, O Lucifer, son of the morning!" In his *Praelectiones* he had used Isaiah frequently for superb examples of parallelistic art and brilliant deployment of metaphors. In lecture 7 he had discoursed on the Hebrew *sheol*, Greek *Hades*, and Latin *Infernum* and their various literary descriptions, explaining how the Hebrew visions of *sheol* grew out of the extensive burial caves and vaults, especially for royalty. "Many of these are still extant in Judea: two in particular are more magnificent than all the rest [notes here give references to two travelers and to Josephus, Strabo, Homer, Pliny, Varro], and are supposed to be the sepulchres of kings. One of these is in Jerusalem and contains twenty-four cells." And then still in lecture 7 he commented on this "great ode" of Isaiah 14.

> Figure to yourselves a vast, dreary, dark, sepulchral cavern, where the Kings of the nations lie, each upon his bed of dust, the arms of each beside him, his sword under his head, and the graves of their numerous [at each point he confirms his images with references to Ezekiel, and to I Maccabees as well as to Isaiah] hosts round about them: Behold! the King of Babylon is introduced, they all rise and go forth to meet him; and receive him as he approaches! "Art thou also come down unto us? Art thou become like unto us? Art thou cut down and withered in thy strength, O thou destroyer of the nations!" (1:165–66)

In all his comments on Isaiah 14 he makes no mention of Milton's stupendous exploitation of Isaiah's lines on the fall of Lucifer but

treats the whole thing as scholars understand it now, a "taunt song"
on the fall of the Babylonian King. In lecture 28 he had included his
own English ode "On the Fate of Tyranny, Isaiah XIV," a stanzaic
rhyming "Pindaric" ode. This poem was much admired, as an out-
standing example in its time of the English "sublime." One passage
runs:

> Hell, from her gulph profound
> Rouses at thine approach; and, all around,
> Her dreadful notes of preparation sound.
> See, at the awful call,
> Her shadowy Heroes all,
> Ev'n mighty Kings, the heirs of empire wide,
> Rising, with solemn state, and slow,
> From their sable thrones below,
> Meet, and insult thy pride.
> What, dost thou join our ghostly train,
> A flitting shadow light, and vain?
> Where is thy pomp, thy festive throng,
> Thy revel dance, and wanton song?
> Proud King! Corruption fastens on thy breast;
> And calls her crawling brood, and bids them share the feast.
> O, Lucifer! thou radiant star;
> Son of the Morn; whose rosy car. . . .

And so on. It is grand in its way, but as Lowth well knew, as soon
as there is meter and rhyme, the parallelism is at risk, or lost. Later,
in his translation of Isaiah, of course he follows the parallel patterns
and therefore, it might be argued, succeeds better. It is an example
of how in conscientious translation this Hebrew structural pattern
preserves itself. The comparable passage runs:

> Hades from beneath is moved because of thee,
>   to meet thee at thy coming:
> He rouseth for thee the mighty dead,
>   all the great chiefs of the earth;
> He maketh to rise up from their thrones,
>   all the Kings of the nations.
> All of them shall accost thee,

and shall say unto thee:
Art thou, even thou too, become weak as we?
    are thou made like unto us?
Is then thy pride brought down to the grave?
    the sound of thy sprightly instruments?
Is the vermin become thy couch,
    and the earthworm thy covering?
How art thou fallen from heaven,
    O Lucifer, son of the Morning!
Art cut down to the earth,
    thou that didst subdue the nations!

In his notes on "Lucifer" he observes how the Hebrew poets take images

> from the most striking parts of nature, from the heavenly bodies, from the sun, moon and stars; which they describe as shining with increased splendor, and never setting . . . : see Is.xxx.26. new heavens and a new earth are created, and a brighter age commences. On the contrary, the overthrow and destruction of kingdoms is represented by opposite images: the stars are obscured, the moon withdraws her light, and the sun shines no more. . . . (2:91)

And typically he gives examples as references—Joel, Amos, Matthew. He notes of this whole poem, called a *mashal* in Hebrew (KJV *proverb*, Lowth *parable* as in the Balaam story), that the Septuagint calls it a *threnos*, or *lamentation*, clearly thereby indicating its genre (a) as poetry, (b) as an elegy. Altogether it is "one of the first and most eminent examples extant of the truly great and beautiful in poetic style" (2:91, 97).

III: Lowth as Critic

In spite of the radical importance of Lowth's biblical studies, some critics now give an oddly grudging and querulous account of him. Hans Frei complains that Lowth avoids the question of narrative truth in the Bible,[23] as though it was not legitimate to write about the poetry. James Kugel objects to Lowth's famous achievement, the

demonstration of parallelism. Lowth had spent considerable effort
in classifying different kinds: chiefly as synonymous, antithetical,
and synthetic. The classification has been followed, perhaps too slav-
ishly, by some subsequent critics.[24] Kugel takes violent objection to
this, assuming that synonymity means *stasis*. He says Lowth conceives of A and B as simultaneous and fails to see that "B must
inevitably be understood as A's *completion*; A, and what's more, B;
not only A, but B; not A, not even B . . . and so forth."[25] But one
must answer that sometimes, certainly, A and B *are* simultaneous:
"When Israel went out of Egypt / the house of Jacob from a strange
people" (Ps. 114:1). Synonyms, moreover, are never *mere* repetition.
Kugel's book is wonderfully learned and informative, but when he
comes to literary criticism, he fails remarkably and cancels out his
own logic. In this long book about biblical poetry, he finally denies it
exists. One can see at times his bias: he has shuddered, he says, to
hear Joseph called "one of the most believable characters in Western
literature," for Joseph, "is no *character* at all, but someone far more
intimately ours."[26] It seems that Kugel is loath to have any of the
Bible considered "literature" or "poetry," and so there is a basic an-
tipathy to Lowth's critical approach. It is really nonsense to deny, as
Kugel does, the difference between poetry and prose in the Bible, and
on this issue Kugel is naive. Literary scholars are well used to the
relativistic problem of defining what poetry is but nevertheless are
absolutely certain of its existence. We would not by any means limit
the power of poetry, either. Kugel feels to call the Bible "poetry"
denigrates it.[27]

Robert Alter has objected to Lowth's "synonymous," and he also
assumes it means *stasis*. He laments the neglect of Herder's comment
that "the two [parallel] members strengthen, heighten, empower
each other."[28] But Lowth himself wrote, "they repeat, they vary, they
amplify" (1:100), and Herder's fine observation develops out of his
study of Lowth. But, in a way, Lowth's classification, while perhaps
of heuristic value, is best finally discarded. When we do practical
analysis, we do best to specify in each case just what the parallelism
consists in, and in the process gain a sense of the immense variety
and suppleness of this "meter," and its art.

But I would insist on the value of returning to the study of
Lowth. Throughout, he interests himself in the phenomenology of
reading, and indeed of criticism. See the passage quoted previously,

"The mind . . . should exert itself to discover, if possible, the connexion between the literal and figurative meanings . . . " (*Lectures* 1:155). He invites us also to exert our minds to discover the specific nature of specific parallelisms and may be forgiven his classification of them as an effort in that direction. Adèle Berlin, in considering response to parallelism in Hebrew verse, brings to bear a very apposite comment of William Empson's. As it happens, Empson was writing about contiguous related statements in Chinese poetry: "such contiguity creates the impression of connectedness and forces the reader to 'consider their relationship for himself' and to 'invent a variety of reasons' to explain it." She adds that with biblical parallelism this is all the more so: "The reader cannot avoid considering the relationship."[29] Indeed the very fact of parallelism, where A and B have elements in common, throws the different elements into relief. Robert Alter also suggests that what we do in reading Hebrew parallel poetry is "note the differences."[30] These are forms of the heightened engagement that occurs in the reading of poetry; much more brain activity comes into play than, say, when we are watching TV.

Lowth's influence is incalculable. He is said to have inspired Sir William Jones's work on Oriental languages which in turn contributed much to German philology and Orientalism. But Lowth's influence was direct on Herder, who more than any other figure can be called the father of Historicism and the Higher Criticism of the Bible. Friedrich Meinecke concludes:

> Lowth's book was perhaps the most intellectually important product of the whole Pre-Romantic movement in England. It was free of all dilettantism and superficiality of taste, and had the indirect result of contributing to the liberation of historical research from the bonds of theology by displaying the purely human and historical content and value of the Bible. It set forth a genuine science of the humanities and gave it new organs.[31]

Herder's *Vom Geist der hebräischen Poesie*,[32] 1783, starts off with a tribute to Lowth and builds in a discursive way on Lowth's concepts, developing Herder's own characteristic and influential notions: that societies develop in infinite variety and each should be studied and evaluated on its own terms; that a society's "primitive" or "folk" poetry is its most precious and characteristic treasure. For him, Hebrew poetry, like the folk balladry of the North whose study he instigated, was one of these treasures, and we owe it our best efforts of historical research. Like Lowth, he insists on bringing the light of history to biblical texts. Lowth had said in the *Lectures* that the critic must "remark as far as possible, the situation and habits of the author, the natural history of his country, and the scene of the poem" (1:139, quoted previously). And again, we must acquaint ourselves with

> the language of this people, their manners, discipline, rites, and ceremonies; we must investigate their inmost sentiments, the manner and connexion of their thoughts; in one word, we must see all things with their eyes, estimate all things by their opinions; we must endeavour as much as possible to read Hebrew as the Hebrews would have read it. (1:113)

This stance of Lowth's leads one to wonder whether he was acquainted with the *Scienza Nuova* (1730) of Giambattista Vico, with its valorization of the humanities as opposed to science, its appreciation of metaphors and poetry as revealing a nation's culture, its assertion that Homer and the Hebrew poets have much in common, that each society should be studied with sympathy and as much as possible in its own terms. It is one of the problems in the history of ideas that Herder in developing the epoch-making concept of Historicism appears to be deeply influenced by Vico, although no direct influence is known.[33] It may be that Lowth himself is the connecting link. Can we know whether Lowth read Vico? With his enormous learning and intellectual curiosity, and his travels on the continent including Italy, it seems altogether probable. Herder invented *Einfühling;* maybe Lowth gave him the idea. Herder's study of Hebrew poetry is more expansive and loosely "appreciative" than Lowth's, but it shows Lowth's influence everywhere. Herder even uses many of the examples Lowth does: the Song of Moses, Isaiah 14, and so on. So the stream of learning developed in Germany, leaving England for a time in an intellectual backwater, till the great learning of the German Bible critics filtered back to England in the nineteenth century.

Lowth's study of Hebrew poetry, let us note in conclusion, drew the endorsement and love of a great Hebrew—and Hebraist—Moses Mendelssohn. In Germany, Mendelssohn reviewed the *Praelectiones,* knew the Isaiah translation, and used Lowth's methods in his own scholarship. In 1781, he sent to Lowth a gift of his own translation of Genesis and Exodus, accompanied, as his biographer tells us, by a letter written in ornate Hebrew. In this genre of letter, the trick is to use as many passages from Scripture as you can. It bore the Hebrew date and read as follows:

> To the Cedar on Lebanon, Prince of Tora and Wisdom, the Priest that is highest among his brethren in the Royal City of London (may God protect it), my Honored Teacher [Kevod rabbi] Lowth (may he be granted children and length of days, Amen) from the hyssop out of the wall [see 1 Kings 5:13], Moses son of Rabbi Mendel of blessed memory [the greeting of] peace.
>
> Wherewith shall I come before thy face [Mic. 6:6] my lord! We who take pleasure in the language of thy country and love her dust [Ps. 102:5]! Wherewith shall we render thanks unto thee for all the good thou hast bestowed upon us by thy loved and cherished books: the one on sacred poetry in general, which I read and which was to my palate like the best wine [Song of Sol. 7:10] and the one of Isaiah's prophecy in particular, which is well known and highly esteemed [and he presents his Genesis and Exodus]. . . . Peace unto thee.[34]

Moses Mendelssohn was also, like Lowth, one of those who believed that man has a particular duty to use his reason—the candle of God, as the Cambridge Platonists used to call it—to illuminate his most important concerns: religion, ethics, scriptures.

Postscript

In 1750 there were earthquakes in London, so severe that Londoners stayed away from the theaters and resorted to the country, and the famous impresario-composer George Frideric Handel was casting about for a new subject to recoup his theater's fortunes. Somehow—the biographers don't tell us how—he settled on a secular poem written by Robert Lowth sometime earlier, *The Judgement of Hercules*, adapted by an unknown librettist and called *The Choice of Hercules*. It is a one-act "Interlude" or "Serenata," for which Handel used some music left over from an aborted play, *Alceste* by Tobias Smollett. The subject is an old fable supposed to be told by Socrates, as Xenophon records, about how the young Hercules was wooed by two abstractions in turn: Sloth (or Pleasure) and Virtue (Hard Work); after each had sung her persuasive best, Hercules chose the strenuous course of Virtue. Lowth writes in imitation of the Spenserian style (Spenser was felt to be a natural or primitive poet), and gives Handel occasion for some fine ensemble singing and orchestration. So far as I know, there is no record of any personal encounter between Lowth and Handel. And yet they were at one point both at Oxford at the same time. Lowth had gone up to New College, Oxford, in 1729, and was presumably there until he left to take up his first clerical post at nearby Overton in 1735. In 1733, Handel, becoming famous, visited Oxford at the invitation of the university vice-chancellor, for the occasion of "an elaborate degree-giving ceremony known as the Publick Act."[35] Handel is said to have been offered an honorary degree, but refused it for unknown reasons. He gave five oratorio performances in the new Sheldonian Theatre, including the première of *Athalia*, the first real oratorio. It dramatizes some of the sensational biblical history of the daughter of Jezebel, material already used in Racine's play *Athalie*. It is hard to imagine that Lowth, with his interest in HB literature, would have stayed away. Handel also conducted his *Acis and Galatea* at Oxford, and some of his anthems were sung in the Sunday service at St. Mary's Church, and he himself played the organ—his organ performances were much acclaimed. Jennens, himself an Oxford man of a slightly earlier generation—Balliol, 1715—had followed Handel to Oxford in order to hear his music. Handel's Oxford visit was a headline event, altogether. So perhaps we can permit ourselves to think that these two heroes of the Bible in English, Handel and Lowth, were aware of each other. They had in common, like two Herculeses, chosen Virtue in the form of Hard Work, one in valiant criticism, the other one in a phenomenal production of great music. And each added a special dimension to the relationship of the Bible to English culture.

Chapter 7

Isaiah in England

When Wordsworth announced his program of writing poetry "in the language really used by men," his friend Coleridge demurred. He said the rustic idiom Wordsworth aimed to reproduce was in fact an idiom shaped by the education the speakers had received, and for them there were "few books familiar but the Bible and the liturgy or hymn book. . . . It is an excellent remark of Dr. Henry More's," he goes on to say, "'that a man of confined education but of good parts, by constant reading of the Bible will naturally form a more winning and commanding rhetoric than those that are learned. . . . '"[1] It is the Bible rather than "nature," Coleridge is arguing, that makes the speech of rural people simple, clear, and vigorous; it is the Bible that counteracts the etiolated conventions of "poetic diction." We have to, surely, grant Coleridge's point: language is not something innate, but something we learn in our particular acculturation, and the effect of the Bible on the English language is ubiquitous, infinite, and incalculable.[2] The effect of the Bible on English literature, however, is sometimes conscious and calculable. And now I propose to examine some effects, such as the conscious imitations of KJV rhetoric, some trends in biblical criticism and biblical translation, and a few of the myriads of biblical strands that are resemanticized and reenergized in our literature.

Christopher Smart, 1722–71, is probably the most notable—and engaging—of the imitators of biblical rhetoric. Smart was particularly enravished with English versions of Hebrew poetry. It was one of his three "passions," the second being the music of his own time—such as Handel's—and the third being the beloved Roman poet Horace. Of Horace, he did some distinguished translations. For the music passion, he appears to aim to follow in the Jennens-Handel path: he composed libretti for two biblical oratorios, one, *Hannah*, 1764, with

music by John Worgan, and the other *Abimelech*, 1768, music by Dr.
Arnold. But his libretti are English metrical versions of the biblical
material, and not admired; and the music is—not Handel. *Messiah*
succeeds and endures because of Handel and because the libretto is
strictly biblical, not—as Herder said—one of your pretty-rhyming
cantatas. Smart also wrote many hymns adapting biblical words into
short stanzaic forms as in the Scottish metrical psalms. He is pre-
sumed not to have studied the original Hebrew; at least he says, "For
I have glorified God in Greek and Latin, the consecrated languages
spoken by the Lord on earth,"[3] a curiously uninformed statement.
Jesus, of course, spoke Aramaic, while, as all the world knows, God
spoke Hebrew. But in some famous and charming poems, Smart
sounds biblical, by his construction of "verses" of varying length without particular meter; and while he doesn't go in for any notable
patterns of paralleling as Isaiah and the Psalms do, he amasses great
series of catalogues in parallel groups:

> For I rejoice like a worm in the rain in him that cherishes and him
>   that tramples.
> For I am ready for the trumpet and the alarm to fight to die and
>   to rise again. . . .
> For I pray God for the professors of the University of Cambridge
>   to attend and to amend. . . .[4]

and the beloved liturgy "Of Jeoffrey, His Cat":

> For I will consider my cat Jeoffrey.
> For he is the servant of the Living God, duly and daily serving
>   him. . . .
> For when he takes his prey he plays with it to give it a chance.
> For one mouse in seven escapes by his dallying. . . .
> For he counteracts the powers of darkness by his electrical skin
>   and glaring eyes.
> For he counteracts the Devil, who is death, by brisking about the
>   life.
> For in his morning orisons he loves the sun and the sun loves
>   him. . . .

> For the Lord commanded Moses concerning the cats at the
>   departure of the Children of Israel from Egypt.
> For every family had one cat at least in the bag. . . .[5]

The poet of the book of Job had expatiated on the quiddity of the horse, and Behemoth (very like a crocodile), and Leviathan (very like a hippopotamus), with wonderfully close observation, full of love, humor, and awe; Smart's celebration of the cat seems to follow this precedent. His appreciation of biblical poetry is further attested by his "Song to David," which acclaims David, by tradition the sweet psalmist of Israel, as the greatest poet of all times. In form, it is English meter, six-line stanzas rhyming *a a b c c b* in ballad-like rhythm. But there are eighty-six stanzas, sorted into numbered sets, which suggests a consciousness of the numerical-acrostic biblical poems such as Psalm 119.

Smart may have known Lowth's *Lectures* and his Isaiah. Certainly Lowth's work was becoming increasingly well known among the *literati*. And meanwhile Bishop Percy's feeling for "primitive" poetry, along with the Germans' feeling for early Hebrew as one of the great "primitive" literatures, was fueling the general interest in the Hebrew language and biblical poetry. It seems to have been something even of a commonplace to appreciate an affinity between Hebrew and English poetry. Byron, for instance, satirizes his bluestocking wife in the character of Donna Inez in his *Don Juan:*

> She knew the Latin—that is, "the Lord's prayer,"
> And Greek—the alphabet—I'm nearly sure. . . .
> She liked the English and the Hebrew tongue,
> And said there was analogy between 'em;
> She proved it somehow out of sacred song,
> But I must leave the proofs to those who've seen 'em. . . .
>   (Canto 1, 13–14)

Byron himself, however, capitalized on the general interest with his poems entitled *Hebrew Melodies,* written before he turned satirical about his wife. The subjects are from the HB, and the poems were composed to be set by I. Nathan to tunes from the religious services of the Jews. They are, of course, in various English meters (such as "She walks in Beauty, like the night . . . ") and reflect no particular influence of Hebrew verse or its translations.

It is Blake who is the most obviously "biblical" of the Romantics, and his case in this respect as in others is most peculiar. The subject of Blake and the Bible demands at least a volume. It runs intermittently through *Fearful Symmetry*, the study of Blake by Northrop Frye, who was uniquely qualified to deal with it; Frye patiently sorts out the all-too-original uses Blake makes of biblical myth. For now, for our context here, we might observe that Blake seems to have known some Hebrew and was probably familiar with Lowth's translation of Isaiah and his commentary. For instance, one of his watercolors illustrates chapter 14 of Isaiah, which Lowth had so especially drawn attention to. It pictures the King of Babylon in Hell: "Hell from Beneath is Moved for Thee," with Isaiah pointing the way—noble, stern, and himself more royal in aspect than the kings. And there is a drawing, "Isaiah Foretelling the Destruction of Jerusalem," with that nobility of mien that is in harmony with Lowth's sense of Isaiah.[6] Blake himself alleges that "the prophets Isaiah and Ezekiel dined with me. . . . "[7] One can only gasp, and hope that he didn't talk as he sometimes wrote: "Old Nobodaddy aloft / Farted and belched and coughed."[8] But it was nevertheless an important encounter, with dinner or without: Lowth had been the first to make it widely known that the prophets were in fact poets, writing according to certain metrical forms; with Blake we have the poet confidently taking on the prophetic office. In this office, in his "prophetic poems," he writes in a manner that imitates the English translation of Hebrew poetry, with lines of irregular length and some occasional intimations of parallelism and a great many biblical figures—as well as his own peculiar invented mythology, which one may not care to decode. His illustrations for the Bible, likewise, one may not care to admire, especially I think if one has a strong sense of the high quality of the texts. But then the short poems are beyond praise. The prophetic voice, the biblical images, have all been transmuted, refined as by a refiner's fire, in the *Songs of Innocence* and *Songs of Experience*. And the superb "Jerusalem"—which may reflect some ideas of the British Israelites[9]—

And did those feet in ancient time
Walk upon England's mountains green?[10]

as set to splendid music by Hubert Parry, has become virtually a national hymn.

Smart and Blake both tried out "poetry" that imitates the verse lines in the English Bible. Later, across the sea, Walt Whitman took up something like prophetic strain and cultivated an irregular verse line, achieving his own kind of resonance and "biblical" tone.[11] But there was at the same period a new movement toward free verse, and the "biblical" line ceases to be felt as "biblical" and merely contributes its looseness to the new genre. None of the biblical imitators, so far as I can see, achieves anything like the eloquent semantic parallelisms of the Psalms and Isaiah, parallelisms that survive translation from the Hebrew. From time to time, a superficially "biblical" style comes up in English. The idiom of 1611 and the sonorous English prose rhythms can be imitated for purposes satirical or serious; if serious, there's a striving for the portentous or homiletic.

Lowth's *Lectures* and his edition of Isaiah remained immensely influential. When at last the Church of England sponsored an official revision in 1870,[12] to be done by two companies, one for the Old Testament, one for the New Testament, Lowth's influence was demonstrated. The New Testament appeared in 1881, and the Old Testament and New Testament together in 1885. Many errors were corrected, and the precedent was set for new and improved versions. Thanks chiefly to Lowth, it was now accepted that Hebrew poetry was indeed poetry, and included the prophets; the new version, at times at least, differentiated the poetry from prose typographically as our modern versions do. But before the 1885 publication, two notable translations of Isaiah had already appeared, due in good part to Lowth's high evaluation of his poetry, and perhaps also to the love for many parts kept current by Handel's *Messiah*. One member of the Old Testament Revision company was Thomas Kelly Cheyne, 1841–1915, who had in 1870 brought out *The Book of Isaiah Chronologically Arranged*, which is said to have initiated adequate scholarship in England for his time. He had studied in Göttingen with the great Ewald, and imbibed the latest German Higher Criticism. He averred that "preconceived theological notions ought to be rigorously excluded from exegesis";[13] in the case of Isaiah, of course, this means that the birth and career of Jesus are not predicted by "a virgin shall conceive" (14:3) or "He shall feed his flock" and so on. He did other still more scholarly versions later; one of 1898 ingeniously indicated the current theory of composite authorship by printing in six different colors![14] Sadly, he later became evangelical in a special way of his own, to a point, his biographer says, beyond sanity.[15]

Meanwhile, Matthew Arnold, utterly convinced that mankind under increasingly democratic and scientific education was becoming increasingly rational and would therefore soon reject all biblical miracles and Christian supernaturalism, labored to show that Christianity and the value of the Bible did not depend on the miraculous or the supernatural. His bailiwick as school inspector had been all Dissenters' schools, all that were not Church of England schools, that is. This gave him an intimate view of the constricted and barren culture of the fundamentalists, with what result we can see in *Culture and Anarchy*. His rounds included also the Jewish schools, and the encounter with them led to an important friendship with the Rothschilds, especially Louisa, Lady de Rothschild, Sir Anthony's wife, née Montefiore. He was deeply impressed with the Jewish Free School in London, which the Rothschilds supported; with the liberal culture and Hebrew studies of Lady de Rothschild and her family; with the family tutor Marcus Kalisch, a man of great piety and learning; and with their friend the scholar Emmanuel Deutsch of the British Museum. It was Deutsch who taught George Eliot Hebrew and served as the model for Mordecai in *Daniel Deronda*. Arnold, like George Eliot and Prime Minister Gladstone, studied Hebrew and was sympathetic with liberal Judaic culture. In the preface to *Culture and Anarchy* Arnold wrote, "The conception which cultivated and philosophical Jews now entertain of Christianity and its Founder, is probably destined to become the one which Christians themselves will entertain."[16] He and Lady de Rothschild shared a particular love for the poetry of Isaiah.

England was at this time moving toward a comprehensive national education; in view of the crippling disputes as to what kind of religion would be taught in government schools, it seemed a likely solution to circumscribe religion and possibly excise the Bible. Arnold in his inspector's report of 1869 urged an element of Bible study in the secular school curriculum. "The Bible is for the child in an elementary school almost his only contact with poetry and philosophy."[17] The Old Testament is the most suitable for literary study, he explains, since it exhibits Hebrew literature in its perfection, while the New Testament purports only "to be a plain record of events, or else epistles . . . [not] aspiring to the literary qualities of poetry, rhythm and eloquence."[18] And he himself set about to encourage the school program with a little book *A Bible Reading for Schools*, comprising the Deutero-Isaiah, or Isaiah 40–66, published in 1872. This was reissued in 1875 for the general reader, with an introduction and some additions; Arnold was then instigated to add Isaiah 1–39, and he published the whole work in 1883 with an introduction.[19] (It is interesting to remember that Moses Mendelssohn in Germany had offered his own translation of the Psalms to the German state schools, to enrich the program and to draw attention to the joint legacy of synagogue and church.)[20] Arnold was generally familiar with the German scholarship and had T. K. Cheyne's version to hand. Unquestionably Cheyne was the better Hebraist, but Arnold had enough Hebrew to follow the scholarship and make the choices. Like Cheyne, and like the revision in progress, Arnold subscribes to minimal change from the KJV. Other things being equal Arnold will give preference to the version of Isaiah as quoted in the New Testament, noting the thirty-four such quotations listed by Gesenius. At times he uses his knowledge of parallel structure to determine the preferred reading. He acclaims Lowth's criticism but deplores his version at points: certainly Lowth's "Speak ye animating words to Jerusalem" is no improvement on "Speak ye comfortably to Jerusalem." He finds that Cheyne, while correct, is insensitive to the KJV style and frequently loses some good rhythm or effect unnecessarily. In his notes, he expects to be acceptable to Anglican, Roman Catholic, or Jew, but he confines himself to the "local and temporary side" of the prophecies—dodging the issue of typology so as not to offend the Christians. But in fact, he can be a good literary critic of the Bible because he has freed himself from typological readings. Altogether, he took pride in his Isaiah. "I rate the value of the operation of poetry and literature on men's minds extremely high," he says in his introduction. "And from no poetry and literature, not even from our own Shakespeare and Milton, great as they are and our own as they are, have I, for my own part, received so much delight as from Homer and Isaiah." And Hebrew poetry can be "preserved and transferred" in a foreign language because of the parallelism, as Homer cannot be.[21] Finally, it seems to me that Arnold's biblical criticism is some of his best *literary* criticism,[22] and his edition of Isaiah is worthy of study. He had been called in the press, for his urbane dealings with religious matters, a "kid-gloved high priest," an "elegant Jeremiah," and he objected vigorously. Jeremiah is the prophet whose "style I admire the *least*,"[23] he said; and certainly in his biblical-literary writings Isaiah is given the preference Lowth accorded it. Arnold's edition and criticism must have contributed to the continuing viability of Isaiah in English culture.

Certainly biblical texts like Isaiah continue to have their effect on English literature, reactivated and resemanticized by the poets. I turn now to how some strands of the biblical web reemerge in poets of the *fin de siècle*, two poets at opposite poles of doctrine who borrow in different ways the energy of the ancient work: the atheist A. E. Housman and the Roman Catholic convert—and Jesuit—Gerard Manley Hopkins.

Housman first, then: he must be one of the most intertextualist of poets, one of the most learned.[24] Even though his output is minuscule in comparison to Milton's, he is like Milton in learning and density of allusion. Housman was Professor of Latin at Cambridge, and the distinguished editor of Manilius, and he liked to keep his scholar persona separate from the poet. But they do connect. The greatest Latinist of his day is indeed the reclusive author of *A Shropshire Lad*. It is curious that many readers are first drawn to Housman in youth, perhaps without any knowledge of the "quotations, references, and echoes" in his poetry. But for the lettered, there is no end to the games of discovery of traces of other texts, sometimes reported singly in letters to the TLS or *Notes and Queries*—a whole library of these has developed.[25] The connections with the classics are extraordinarily rich; I am not qualified to trace and evaluate these, although my experience of Virgil, Horace, and Catullus is enough to convince me of a kind of kinship in the *lapidary* quality of the verse; and in metrics. I believe, though I have no idea how to go about an analysis, that Housman's appreciation of quantitative patterns in Latin verse is at work in his English verse, as an overlay of the English accentual patterns. He can, to put it minimally, as one critic does, "make judicious use of a pause or a long syllable."[26] Other connections with the classics are easier to trace: like-mindedness with Sophocles, with the melancholy lyrics of the Greek Anthology, with Lucretius, with Horace; innumerable mythological allusions proper; two imitations of a famous poem by Sappho; a handful of superb translations; the Greek

habit of compound adjectives: *many-venomed* in the Mithridates poem
is Greek *polypharmakos*. And here's an interesting thing for intertextu-
alists: the assuredly calculated fact that the number of poems
Housman published in his lifetime is precisely the number of Horace's poems—one hundred and four.

But these poems have thousands of demonstrable overtones of
earlier texts from all through the Western tradition: besides the clas-
sics, the Bible ubiquitously, Shakespeare, ballads, folk songs, Milton,
Pope, Gray, Goldsmith, Dr. Johnson, Scott, Blake, Byron, Keats, Ten-
nyson, Matthew Arnold (many echoes and specific phrases),
Christina Rossetti, Andrew Lang, Charles Kingsley, Rudyard
Kipling, Robert Bridges! We know he loved the little French folk song
"Nous n'irons plus au bois" on the evidence of an exquisite translation: "We'll to the woods no more." From German, there is especially
Heine, whose importance to him Housman acknowledges, and
there's a whole set of connections there: the use of folk ballad forms
and subjects, the astringent wit, the ironic use of the Bible, and a
hostile attitude to Jehovah.

The consideration of his uses of the Bible seems to invite definition of this hostility, and his religious position in general. He once
declared, in answer to an inquiry,

> I was brought up in the Church of England and in the High
> Church party, which is much the best religion I have ever come
> across. But Lemprière's Classical Dictionary, which fell into my
> hands when I was eight, attached my affections to paganism. I
> became a deist at thirteen and an atheist at twenty-one.[27]

One of his poems, "New Year's Eve,"[28] a sort of God-is-dead statement about "divinities disannointed," he wanted to suppress not for
its doctrine, but for its style. His brother Laurence reports that he
said:

> It smacked too much of the Swinburnian style which he had
> abandoned. He wrote it, he said, in his twentieth year. "I was
> then a deist." "And now," [Laurence asked] "what do you call
> yourself—an agnostic?" "No," he said decisively. "I am an athe-
> ist." He then went on to say that he thought the Church of

England the best religion ever invented; it was less disturbing than other forms, and eliminated "so much Christian nonsense."[29]

In another context he describes himself as a "High-Church atheist."[30] Laurence further reports:

Belief in immortality was quite unnecessary, he said, for good morals. The Hebrews had a higher code of morals than the Egyptians, and did not allow themselves to be perverted from nonbelief in a future life by Egyptian superstition.[31]

As a schoolboy he had written for the school magazine about a people—

who worshipped a god called Goodness Gracious, who originally demanded the sacrifice of young children. Then when babies ran short, someone had the idea of substituting kid-dolls which made a screaming noise in the fire; and finding that these satisfied him equally well, they experimented in a cheaper kind; and finally (as nothing made any difference) they sacrificed whatever they could spare best and would miss least. At the date when the story opened they were piously sacrificing a diseased potato-crop, which the god seemed to like as well as anything.[32]

He rejects that Victorian label *agnostic,* and he insists on *atheism,* a positive hostility to the cosmic Establishment. One does not *know* ultimate reality, true, but one knows the human condition is bad:

Who made the world I cannot tell;
'Tis made, and here am I in hell.
My hand, though now my knuckles bleed,
I never soiled with such a deed—[33]

To be anything but hostile would be disingenuous: "high heaven and earth ail from the prime foundation";[34] there is "iniquity on high," on the part of "Whatever brute and blackguard made the world."[35]

The troubles of our proud and angry dust
Are from eternity, and shall not fail.[36]

These anti-Establishment statements are in a kind of Victorian tradition of blasphemy, a genre that flourishes only when there is a strong orthodoxy to outrage. "Thy Kingdom shall pass, Galilean," sang Swinburne, and he taunted the lord God as rudely as Elijah taunted the priests of Baal. Fitzgerald behind the mask of Omar is also on the attack:

What! out of senseless Nothing to provoke
A conscious Something to resent the yoke
    Of unpermitted Pleasure, under pain
Of Everlasting Penalties, if broke!
        . . . Oh, the sorry trade!
O Thou, who Man of Baser Earth didst make
And ev'n with Paradise devise the Snake
    For all the Sin wherewith the Face of Man
Is blackened—Man's forgiveness give—and take!

I think in Housman's case it is fair to cite the biographical element: his beloved and devout mother, to whom he was very close, died when he was twelve, *on his birthday*. This looks very much like malice. His great love—and he believed one loved only once—was unrequited.[37] His mother had nurtured him in the Christian tradition on extensive Bible reading and memorization. His uncompromising scientific mind, exercised in youth on astronomy and its vast spaces, obliged him to forgo Christian dogma. He made in his "Introductory Lecture" for University College, London, a statement of the rationale for the pursuit of knowledge:

It may be urged that man stands today in the position of one who has been reared from his cradle as the child of a noble race and the heir to great possessions, and who finds at his coming of age that he has been deceived alike as to his origin and his expectations; that he neither springs of the high lineage he fancied, nor will inherit the vast estate he looked for, but must put

off his towering pride, and contract his boundless hopes, and
begin the world anew from a lower level; and this, it may be
urged, comes of pursuing knowledge.

But he goes on to say, in nicely minimal terms:

> It is and it must be in the long run better for man to see things
> as they are than to be ignorant of them. . . .[38]

The place of poetry in this sorry scheme is grandly explained as
a kind of inoculation, in "Terence, this is stupid stuff":

> . . . the stuff I bring for sale
> Is not so brisk a brew as ale:
> Out of a stem that scored the hand
> I wrung it in a weary land.
> But take it: if the smack is sour,
> The better for the embittered hour;
> It should do good to heart and head
> When your soul is in my soul's stead. . . .[39]

And there's a straight borrowing from Job 16:4: "if your soul were in
my soul's stead, I could heap up words against you. . . . " The allusion, in the simplest vocabulary, is a deft clarification of meaning; the
speaker is in a bad way, sought out by programmed misfortune.
Poetry can make it in some degree supportable. Or poetry can be a
kind of armor, as in this:

> I to my perils
>   Of cheat and charmer
>   Came clad in armour
>   By stars benign.
> Hope lies to mortals
>   And most believe her,
>   But man's deceiver
>   Was never mine.
>
> The thoughts of others
>   Were light and fleeting,

> Of lovers' meeting
>> Or luck or fame.
> Mine were of trouble,
>> And mine were steady,
>> So I was ready
>> When trouble came.[40]

And at one point in his life, where his honesty is particularly guaranteed by his great love for the members of his family, he writes to his sister Kate Symons on the death of her son in battle in 1915:

> I do not know that I can do better than send you some verses that I wrote many years ago; because the essential business of poetry, as it has been said, is to harmonise the sadness of the universe, and it is somehow more sustaining and healing than prose.[41]

There are here overtones of the defense of poetry by Matthew Arnold, whom Housman revered, and Arnold's statement that poetry can console and sustain. The poem in question is the perfect little elegy "Illic Jacet."[42] For Housman, the "sadness of the universe" is a given.

> But this unlucky love should last
>> When answered passions thin to air;
> Eternal fate so deep has cast
>> Its sure foundation of despair.[43]

And the literature of the Bible—it may seem odd—was his greatest literary resource in harmonizing the sadness. The most overt instances are witty perversions of the sense of scripture:

> When Israel out of Egypt came
>> Safe in the sea they trod;
> By day in cloud, by night in flame,
>> Went on before them God. . . .

> Ascended is the cloudy flame,
>> The mount of thunder dumb;

The tokens that to Israel came,
  To me they have not come.

I see the country far away
  Where I shall never stand;
The heart goes where no footstep may
  Into the promised land. . . .[44]

For him as for Moses on Mount Pisgah, the promised land is a forbidden land.

He remembers Isaiah 55, and the bold metaphor of the voice of the huckster: "Ho, every one that thirsteth, come ye to the waters, and he that hath no money; come ye, buy, and eat; yea, come, buy wine and milk without money and without price. . . . Incline your ear, and come unto me: hear, and your soul shall live. . . . " Housman's version, presumably autobiographical, addresses "forbidden" waters:

Ho, everyone that thirsteth
  And hath the price to give,
Come to the stolen waters,
  Drink and your soul shall live.

Come to the stolen waters,
  And leap the guarded pale,
And pull the flower in season
  Before desire shall fail.

It shall not last for ever,
  No more than earth and skies;
But he that drinks in season
  Shall live before he dies.[45]

The perversion of Isaiah's joy is accomplished with aid of a borrowing from Proverbs ("stolen waters") and one from Ecclesiastes ("Desire shall fail").

"The Carpenter's Son" represents a human Jesus, a very Victorian subject novelized by George Moore in *The Brook Kerith*.

Here hang I, and right and left
Two poor fellows hang for theft:
All the same's the luck we prove,
Though the midmost hangs for love.[46]

And there is an ironic "Easter Hymn":

If in that Syrian garden, ages slain,
You sleep, and know not you are dead in vain,
Nor even in dreams behold how dark and bright
Ascends in smoke and fire by day and night
The hate you died to quench and could but fan,
Sleep well and see no morning, son of man.

But if, the grave rent and the stone rolled by,
At the right hand of majesty on high
You sit, and sitting so remember yet
Your tears, your agony and bloody sweat,
Your cross and passion and the life you gave,
Bow hither out of heaven and see and save.[47]

Here the "smoke and fire by day and night," the holy sign of God,
have become the sign of hate and war. "But if," the second stanza
hypothesizes, "*But if*"—and all the evidence is against it, and the end
is a bitter irony. No one sees and saves.

Housman's recurrent motifs are anti-Christian-doctrine; Death
is repeatedly a sleep, rest, the end of all—as in "For My Funeral," a
kind of pagan prayer:

O thou that from thy mansion
  Through time and place to roam,
Dost send abroad thy children,
  And then dost call them home,

That men and tribes and nations
  And all thy hand hath made
May shelter them from sunshine
  In thine eternal shade:

We now to peace and darkness
   And earth and thee restore
Thy creature that thou madest
   And wilt cast forth no more.[48]

"The Immortal Part" says it with the wittiest irony, that "the immortal part" is not the *soul* as in popular theology. Both soul *and* body, the poet says,

   shall do my will
To-day while I am master still,
And flesh and soul, now both are strong,
Shall hale the sullen slaves along,

Before this fire of sense decay,
This smoke of thought blow clean away,
And leave with ancient night alone
The stedfast and enduring bone.[49]

What is in popular theology the pilgrimage to the promised land is the "fool's-errand to the grave."[50] Some of the most typical wit goes to sly digs at the power of the Most High as in the famous "Jubilee" poem: "God save the Queen," we living sing. . . .

   Get you the sons your fathers got,
   And God will save the Queen.[51]

Or in the "Epitaph on an Army of Mercenaries": "What God abandoned, these defended, and saved the sum of things for pay."[52]
   Instead of the Genesis view of creation as "good," Housman sees "the primal fault."[53] In a curious poem he takes "God" as an arbitrary cultural construct:

   The laws of God, the laws of man,
   He may keep that will and can;
   Not I: let God and man decree
   Laws for themselves and not for me. . . .

And how am I to face the odds
Of man's bedevilment and God's?
I, a stranger and afraid
In a world I never made.[54]

This last affords a significant typical example of his use of actual
biblical texts, here an echo of Psalm 119, and as usual with his reading of Psalms he prefers the PB version of Coverdale: "I am a stranger
upon earth: O hide not thy commandments from me."[55]

One survey tabulates about two hundred uses of the Bible.[56] As
one might expect he draws especially on those books most obviously
sympathetic: Ecclesiastes, Proverbs, Job. But Coverdale's Psalms is
the book most used, about forty times, and this perhaps is not surprising; for there is very little doctrine in the Psalms, and a great deal
of human experience, *de profundis*. But then, it turns out, the range
of reference otherwise is astonishingly broad: Genesis, Exodus, Levit-
icus, Numbers, Joshua, Judges, Samuel, Kings, Chronicles, Ezra,
Isaiah (most frequent of the prophets), Jeremiah, Ezekiel, Daniel,
Amos, Micah, Zechariah, and the apocryphal Ecclesiasticus.[57] And
this pagan poet draws liberally on all four Gospels, Acts, most of the
Epistles, and Revelation. No doubt, there are further uncountable
references. In 1934, Housman's friend John Sparrow published an
essay "Echoes in the Poetry of A. E. Housman."[58] Housman (who did
not die till 1936) in a letter to Sparrow refers to this with his custom-
ary lovable acid:

Some of the plagiarisms on your list I thought imaginary and
non-existent, but a much greater number escaped your notice,
and in particular I see that you are not such a student of the Bible
as I am.[59]

Number 48 of *A Shropshire Lad* affords a good exhibit of how
biblical and religious material gets used.

Be still, my soul, be still; the arms you bear are brittle,
    Earth and high heaven are fixt of old and founded strong.

Think rather,—call to thought, if now you grieve a little,
   The days when we had rest, O soul, for they were long.

Men loved unkindness then, but lightless in the quarry
   I slept and saw not; tears fell down, I did not mourn;
Sweat ran and blood sprang out and I was never sorry:
   Then it was well with me, in days ere I was born.

Now, and I muse for why and never find the reason,
   I pace the earth, and drink the air, and feel the sun.
Be still, be still, my soul; it is but for a season:
   Let us endure an hour and see injustice done.

Ay, look: high heaven and earth ail from the prime foundation;
   All thoughts to rive the heart are here, and all are vain:
Horror and scorn and hate and fear and indignation—
   Oh why did I awake? when shall I sleep again?[60]

First, it has been observed that the opening line echoes not the
Bible but a nineteenth-century hymn:

Be still, my soul: The Lord is on thy side,
Bear patiently the cross of grief and pain. . . .
Be still my soul: the hour is hastening on
When we shall be forever with the Lord,
When disappointment, grief, and fear are gone."[61]

This was a popular hymn of the time, and Housman, typically, re-
verses the Christian-doctrinal point: Be comforted, not because you
will soon be in heaven, but because life will soon cease, forever. The
"arms" is a popular nineteenth-century metaphor, from "Onward
Christian Soldiers" to the Salvation Army; here, instead of armor
potent against evil, it is armor of no avail against an entrenched
cosmic Establishment. The word *quarry* brings a nice point to light.
The word does not occur in the KJV in this metaphorical sense:
Cruden lists only two uses, in the plural, and they are literal. Isaiah
51:1 in the KJV reads:

> Hearken to me, ye that follow after righteousness, ye that seek
> the Lord: look unto the rock *whence* ye are hewn, and to the hole
> of the pit *whence* ye are digged.

In the Revision of 1885, the translators brightly hit upon *quarry* for
hole of the pit, and it seems to me clear that Housman kept up with
the new Bible, fastened on this excellent form of the metaphor, and
developed it elegantly. The poem is part of *A Shropshire Lad*, 1896.
(*Quarry* is retained in the NEB and the Anchor.) In the poem, comfort
is to be found in the shortness of life compared to the length of time
before birth and after death. The three stages are those of Ecclesiastes
4:1–3:

> So I returned, and considered all the oppressions that are done
> under the sun: and behold the tears of such as were oppressed,
> and they had no comforter. . . . Wherefore I praised the dead
> which are already dead more than the living which are yet alive.
> Yea, better is he than both they, which hath not yet been, who
> hath not seen the evil work that is done under the sun.

The note of Ecclesiastes is caught up again in the last stanza:

> All thoughts to rive the heart are here, and *all are vain.* . . .

Ecclesiastes is a book that is deeply Hellenized, and the theme of the
three stages occurs also in Sophocles' *Oedipus Coloneus*, in one of the
choruses, which Housman translated:

> What man is he that yearneth
>   For length unmeasured of days?
> Folly mine eye discerneth
>   Encompassing all his ways. . . .
> Thy portion I esteem the highest,
>   Who was not ever begot;
> Thine next, being born who diest
>   And straightway again art not.[62]

We have some noteworthy solid information about the writing
of this poem, moreover. Laurence Housman tells us that the line "All
thoughts to rive the heart are here, and all are vain" was not easily
achieved. The word *rive* was the eighth tested for that place, after *vex,
plague, tear, wrench, rend, break,* and *pierce.*[63] One is half inclined to
imagine in this case that other self of A. E. Housman, the great
learned editor and emendator of classical texts, faced with a manu-
script lacuna of a certain length, considering the spectrum of possibilities—and he knows the whole spectrum, being so broadly familiar
with so much literature—testing each one, till he finds at last the
"right" one, the one which best satisfies the sense, which best answers to the sound pattern in the poem, not only for the right beat
but also, as I think, as it would happen in Latin verse, to the demand
of *quantity. Rive is* best: it has of course the one syllable required; it
is as strong or stronger than any of the others; it eschews the commonplace of *wrench, wring,* and *break;* it avoids the pettiness of *vex*
and *plague;* it is more radical than *tear, rend,* or *pierce.*

Professor Housman wrote letters of recommendation that often
seem understated; when he appears to give a scholar the accolade,
he says he is "accurate."[64] Housman as scholar plumed himself, with
justice I understand, on his *accuracy,* and he exercised the most withering scorn on inaccurate scholarship. His poetic works bear utterly
unobtrusively the marks of his scholarship, I believe, not least in this
matter of *accuracy.* The poems repeatedly hit the nail on the head.
The poems, like the scholarship, display impeccable logic, a perfect
correctness, consistency, decorum, precision, wit, epigrams, the
most exquisite rhythms, and a steadfast refusal to obscure, palliate,
or flatter anyone or anything. The rhetoric against God in the poetry
is similar to the rhetoric against bad critics in the prose. The poet *is*
the scholar.

But there is that curious fact that the unlearned are drawn to
Housman's poems. Are these poems *intertextual* for the soldiers who
carried them about, for the thoughtful adolescent? Milton, the greatest of learned poets, wrote in a learned, consciously allusive idiom,
but Housman's poems are common people's poems, nearly all in
popular easy ballad meter, always idiomatic, colloquial, homely English, with an occasional latinate word resonantly juxtaposed to the
Anglo-Saxon monosyllables. Gerard Manley Hopkins is one of our
canonized poets, and yet Housman objects to him, for "doing vio-

lence" to the language;[65] this serves to remind us of where Housman aimed, and succeeded: perfectly colloquial, perfectly idiomatic. And the poems are *seamless;* the allusions do not announce themselves or break the surface. How then does Horace, or Shakespeare, or Heine, or the Bible, *work* in the poem? It is curious to think how thin and drab Housman's lovely atheism would be without the Bible. Marlow has a hunch: "he preserves," he says "unimpaired the primitive energy of words";[66] I propose—with some trepidation—that he somehow also preserves unimpaired the energy of the great texts of which the poems show cognizance. I think he is due for a reevaluation upward, in that this seamless poetry does in fact use so large a part of the spectrum of literary tradition. He domesticates innumerable luminous moments of literary experience, he makes them freshly available, he recycles them. His fine body of nonsense verse is a clue to his poise, and irony; his parodies are part of his mastery of the tradition, the negation of Anxiety, and the fact that he was often parodied suggest his reach forward into the future—in the infinite diachronic and synchronic web of semiosis.

There is another aspect of this traditionary art: In the work of harmonizing the sadness of the world, it is a great thing to find we are not alone.

> As I gird on for fighting
>   My sword upon my thigh
> I think on old ill fortunes
>   Of better men than I.[67]

Or:

> Others, I am not the first,
> Have willed more mischief than they durst:
> If in the breathless night I too
> Shiver now, 'tis nothing new.[68]

Or in "On Wenlock Edge":

> 'Twould blow like this through holt and hanger
>   When Uricon the city stood:
> 'Tis the old wind in the old anger,
>   But then it threshed another wood.

> Then, 'twas before my time, the Roman
>   At yonder heaving hill would stare:
> The blood that warms an English yeoman,
>   The thoughts that hurt him, they were there.
>   . . . .
> Then 'twas the Roman, now 'tis I.[69]

The myriad echoes of ancient and recent texts become in themselves a kind of intertextual statement of kinship. Then 'twas Sappho, now 'tis I. Then 'twas the Hebrew King David, now 'tis I. So it is that the poet—in Carlyle's words—"stands ever compassed about with so great a cloud of witnesses and brothers."

One can hardly imagine a poet more unlike Housman than Gerald Manley Hopkins, but they were more or less contemporaries as practicing poets: Housman's *Shropshire Lad* was being written in the years before 1896; Hopkins flourished in the decade before his early death in 1889 (though his poetry was not published till 1918); they both produced a small body of short poems very finely wrought; they were both learned and self-conscious artists. But where Housman is perfectly colloquial in commonplace meters, Hopkins is wildly original and a brilliant executant of that almost impossible form, the Petrarchan sonnet. As Housman said, he "does violence" to the language, and to meter. And Hopkins is at the opposite pole from atheist Housman—he is one of the great English religious poets. While Housman's remarkably pervasive use of the Bible seems to demand an explanation, Hopkins as a Christian, Roman Catholic convert, and Jesuit might be legitimately expected to have a professional and proprietary interest in the Bible. In an early poem, he writes:

> He hath abolished the old drouth,
> And rivers run where all was dry,
> The field is sopped with merciful dew.
> He hath put a new song in my mouth,
> The words are old, the purport new
> And taught my lips to quote this word
> That I shall live, I shall not die,
> But I shall when the shocks are stored
> See the salvation of the Lord.[70]

The challenge runs recurrently in the Psalms and Isaiah: "Sing a new song unto the Lord,"[71] a challenge that religious poets and musicians have loved to rise to through the ages. It is a challenge that Hopkins met with such astounding virtuosity that he shaped a new poetry for the twentieth century. Even in this modest little poem, the new and the old are interlaced: there are the figures from the Psalms, of drought and saving water—a very Near Eastern figure hardly as meaningful in damp green England where Hopkins lived—and of the harvest of souls, from the HB but elaborately developed in the CB, and there is a fine new Hopkinsy word *sopped*, and his muscular forthrightness.

There is another interesting and vivid early poem where Hopkins tries out, as it were, the Browningesque genre of dramatic monologue. This is "A Soliloquy of One of the Spies Left in the Wilderness":

Who is this Moses? who made him, we say,
To be a judge and ruler over us?
He slew the Egyptian yesterday. To-day
   In hot sands perilous
He hides our corpses dropping by the way
   Wherein he makes us stray.[72]

It is a brilliant expansion, it seems to me, of the "murmuring" of the Children of Israel, what Moses had to put up with in the wilderness, which is vivid, dramatic, and human enough in the original. In the last stanza, the incident is deftly moralized in the Christian-typological way: the "murmurer" defects from the pilgrimage and falls into a soul-sickness.

One might wonder whether if Hopkins had been raised a Roman Catholic, rather than becoming a convert at twenty, his poetry would have so many biblical echoes. For Protestantism is so much more biblical than Catholicism, and undoubtedly the Anglican services through his youth supplied him as they did Housman with a bank of biblical memories to draw on, more than the Catholic services would. The main body of his poetry moves more on Catholic themes than Anglican: on vocation, on the Eucharist, on medieval philosophy, on pastoral care, on the Virgin Mary. But of course as a Christian

and a priest he naturally draws much more on the CB than the HB.
One of his few HB subjects is thoroughly typologized in the Christian
manner: "Barnfloor and Winepress"[73] is taken from the vivid account
in 2 Kings 6 of the famine in Samaria so dreadful that people are
turning cannibal, and the King, in sackcloth, is unable to relieve
them. "And he said, If the Lord do not help thee, whence shall I help
thee? Out of the barnfloor, or out of the winepress?"—Hopkins uses
this as the epigraph for the poem. (At this period, he quotes the KJV
rather than the Catholic Douay. He gives the reference as 2 Kings
6:27; the Douay would call it 4 Kings. And the Douay has *save* rather
than *help*.) The poem takes the usual Christian view that what the
Hebrew leader could not do, Christ has done:

> At morn we found the heavenly Bread,
> And on a thousand Altars laid,
> Christ our Sacrifice is made. . . .
> Now in our altar-vessels stored
> Is the sweet Vintage of our Lord.

Another early poem *"Nondum"*[74] (meaning "not yet") has an epigraph from Isaiah: "Verily Thou art a God that hidest Thyself" (45:15.
Again, the version quoted is KJV. Douay has "Verily thou art a hidden God."), and the poem runs a course of feeling parallel to that of
Psalm 42, which begins "As the hart panteth after the water brooks,
so panteth my soul after thee, O God," and speaks of the desolation
of feeling cut off from God. Hopkins begins,

> God, though to Thee our psalm we raise
> No answering voice comes from the skies. . . .

and proceeds, echoing the psalm "Deep calls to deep," and ends like
the psalm in quiet hope. This is not one of Hopkins's best poems—it
is vastly inferior to the psalm itself—but it shows Hopkins finding a
voice and a model in HB poetry.

At one point, in one of the terrible times when he feels
frustrated—or worse—in his calling, he is reading Jeremiah and
recognizes in the pathetic eloquence of Jeremiah a voice for his own
suffering. This time he quotes the epigraph passage in the Vulgate,
Catholic-wise:

Justus quidem tu es, Domine, si disputem tecum: verumtamen
justa loquar ad te: Quare via impiorum prosperantur?

and indeed the poem itself takes off from the Douay version rather
than the KJV. KJV reads: "Righteous *art* thou, O Lord, when I plead
with thee . . . " while the Douay has: "Thou indeed, O Lord, art just,
if I plead with thee . . . " (12:1).[75] The prophet is pleading with God
as though in a law court, and this is expanded in the elegance of a
Petrarchan sonnet—and ends with a prayer.

> Thou art indeed just, Lord, if I contend
> With thee; but, sir, so what I plead is just.
> Why do sinners' ways prosper? and why must
> Disappointment all I endeavour end?
>
> Wert thou my enemy, O thou my friend,
> How wouldst thou worse, I wonder, than thou dost
> Defeat, thwart me? Oh, the sots and thralls of lust
> Do in spare hours more thrive than I that spend,
>
> Sir, life upon thy cause. See, banks and brakes
> Now, leaved how thick! laced they are again
> With fretty chervil, look, and fresh wind shakes
>
> Them; birds build—but not I build; no, but strain,
> Time's eunuch, and not breed one work that wakes.
> Mine, O thou lord of life, send my roots rain.

It is a prayer, it is a *cri de coeur*, and yet it is at the same time a fine
explication of the passage from Jeremiah that adds to one's understanding of the original text. Indeed, it seems that most of his poems
are in fact prayers.

> God rest him all road ever he offended.
> . . . .
> Have, get, before it cloy,
> Before it cloud, Christ, lord, and sour with sinning.
> . . . .
> He fathers forth whose beauty is past change: Praise Him.

This is indeed art in the service of religion, so successfully that it inclines one in favor of both. Hopkins stands in the line of some of the great translators of the KJV and the great seventeenth-century devotional poets: Donne, Traherne, Vaughan, and Herbert especially. And there is furthermore an undertaking of Roman Catholic thought—of Duns Scotus and of Aquinas—that he turns into a sacramental celebration of nature. Medieval "quiddity" becomes for him "inscape," that principle by which all things are so much themselves, and man is God's "clearest-selvèd spark." His intense joy in "dappled things . . . , all things counter, original, spare, strange," is close in spirit to the mode of Job 38–41, the Voice from the Whirlwind hymning the marvels of creation. Hopkins reverences also the varieties of the things men do and make: "all trades, their gear and tackle and trim." The sonnet "God's Grandeur" updates Hebrew and medieval theology.

> The world is charged with the grandeur of God.
>   It will flame out, like shining from shook foil;
>   It gathers to a greatness, like the ooze of oil
> Crushed. Why do men then now not reck his rod?
> Generations have trod, have trod, have trod;
>   And all is seared with trade; bleared, smeared with toil;
>   And wears man's smudge and shares man's smell: the soil
> Is bare now, nor can foot feel, being shod.
> And for all this, nature is never spent;
>   There lives the dearest freshness deep down things;
> And though the last lights off the black West went
>   Oh, morning, at the brown brink eastward, springs—
> Because the Holy Ghost over the bent
>   World broods with warm breast and with ah! bright wings.[76]

The conceptions are from contemporary technology: the world is *charged* with the grandeur of God as with electricity; it flames out as light does from moving tinfoil; it stores tremendous power, as the pressure from rocks sends Texas oil up in "gushers."[77] With all this power so evident, why do we not now "reck his rod"?—*rod*, the KJV HB word for *staff* or *rule*. And the answer is given in lines eerily prophetic of our present ecological disasters: "all is seared with trade; bleared, smeared with toil," and we are, as it were, out of touch with God. But at the *volta*, the *turn*, comes the hope and faith in God, "Because"—and the Holy Ghost is envisioned *brooding* over the world, like the spirit of God *brooding* over creation in Genesis 1, and like the descending dove of the CB. This too is a perfect Petrarchan sonnet: the octave for the world and man, the sestet for God and the doctrine. With Hopkins as with Herbert, this difficult Italian form becomes a spiritual exercise.

In a masterpiece of his mature poetry he has taken possession of and transmuted the brilliance of Isaiah 55, the selfsame passage—as I believe—that Housman so elegantly subverted, "Ho, everyone that thirsteth. . . . " The merchant in the bazaar calls attention to the great bargain he offers.

The Starlight Night

Look at the stars! look, look up at the skies!
  O look at all the fire-folk sitting in the air!
  The bright boroughs, the circle-citadels there!
Down in dim woods the diamond delves! the elves'-eyes!
The grey lawns cold where gold, where quick-gold lies!
  Wind-beat whitebeam! airy abeles set on a flare!
  Flake-doves sent floating forth at a farmyard scare!—
Ah well! it is all a purchase, all is a prize.

Buy then! bid then!—What?—Prayer, patience, alms, vows.
Look, look: a May-mess, like on orchard boughs!
  Look! March-bloom, like on mealed-with-yellow sallows!
These are indeed the barn; withindoors house
The shocks. This piece-bright paling shuts the spouse
  Christ home, Christ and his mother and all his hallows.[78]

The huckster calls attention to his goods and with great effect runs over their attractions (in this case they are the same ones that Psalm 19 celebrates, "The heavens declare the glory of God"). He falls back into

Ah well! it is all a purchase, all is a prize.

This poem again is a perfectly constructed Petrarchan sonnet, and the *volta* in line 9 turns us to the actual transaction. "Buy then! bid then!" and as if in answer to a question the huckster quotes the price: "Prayer, patience, alms, vows." Like any salesman, he quickly reverts to exclaiming on the beauty of the deal, which is, in a figure, the beauty of nature, which is, for Hopkins, incontrovertible Revelation. And then he says, this is the real thing: "These are indeed the barn; withindoors house the shocks"—this is the real harvest as of souls saved. "Incline your ear," Isaiah had said in his bargaining passage, "and come unto me: hear and your soul shall live; and I will make an everlasting covenant with you. . . . " And Hopkins in his sonnet ends by offering the everlasting prize, "Christ home, Christ and his mother and all his hallows." It is like Jesus using monetary terms to explain spiritual things for us hopelessly worldly creatures: "Lay not up for yourself treasure upon earth, where the moth and dust doth corrupt. . . . " The Isaiah passage (and the Hopkins poem) catch us because our ears will generally prick up for a bargain.

So it is that an ancient voice from a Near Eastern bazaar, not so very unlike that of the used-car dealer, is reactivated by the new poet. "Anxiety of Influence" and the "Burden of the Past" have been literary-critical themes widely explored in our time. But there is another side to it—the enabling and enfranchising power of the past, of tradition. Hopkins and Housman both *say things* by means of the Bible that they couldn't have said without it. The fact that they say such different things suggests not the political restraints of a tradition but rather its enabling power. Moreover, the Bible itself is nothing if not multiglossial; in spite of what religionists may say, there is not much consistency. Society has a lot to lose in letting go this long, varied, and peculiar text. It would be a deprivation not to be acquainted with Moses, say. When the Deuteronomist concludes his account of Moses' death, he says, "And there arose not a prophet since in Israel like unto Moses." We can add that there's nobody like him in any other literature or history, either. The poetry too is unique and one of the world's great literary monuments. With its moving semantic rhythms and the physicality of the figures of speech, it touches us at many levels of being. Coleridge said, "In the Bible there is more that *finds* me than I have experienced in all other books put together."[79] We are the richer, the stronger, the more connected for knowing it, as we live and move and have our being in this great web of semiosis.

Notes

Chapter 1

1. "Organic Filaments," in *Sartor Resartus*, bk. 3, chap. 8.
2. "Voltaire," in *Critical and Miscellaneous Essays*, vol. 26 of *The Works of Thomas Carlyle*, Edinburgh ed. (New York: Charles Scribner's Sons, 1903), 1:399.
3. Ibid., 396.
4. *Le Plaisir du texte* (Paris: Editions de Seuil, 1973), 10. My paraphrase.
5. Barthes, "From Work to Text," quoted in Leonard Orr, *Problems and Poetics of the Nonaristotelian Novel* (Lewisburg: Bucknell University Press; London and Toronto: Associated University Presses, 1991), 129.
6. *Le Plaisir du texte,* 100. My translation.
7. Georges Mounin, "L'araignée n'a pas une image positive," quoted in *The Semiotic Web 1989,* ed. Thomas A. Sebeok and Jean Umiker-Sebeok (Berlin and New York: Mouton de Gruyter, 1990), x.
8. Robert E. Innes, *Semiotics: An Introductory Anthology* (Bloomington: Indiana University Press, 1985), xi, xv.
9. Yuri M. Lotman and Boris A. Uspensky, quoted in Orr, *Problems and Poetics,* 126.
10. From 1986 to now. See note 7.
11. Orr, *Problems and Poetics,* 126.
12. See Heinz S. Bluhm, " 'Fyve Sundry Interpreters': The Sources of the First Printed English Bible," *Huntington Library Quarterly* 39 (1976):107–16.
13. Quoted in "English Versions of the Bible 1525–1611," in *Cambridge History of the Bible* (Cambridge: Cambridge University Press, 1963), 3:145.
14. See "British Israelites," in *Encyclopedia Judaica* (New York: Macmillan, 1972), 4:1382. As a child in Western Canada I encountered adherents of the sect. In the United States, it appears to have been adapted into Mormonism.
15. See, for example, Sacvan Bercovitch, *The Puritan Origins of the American Self* (New Haven: Yale University Press, 1975).
16. Isaiah 28:15: "Because ye have said, we have made a covenant with death, and with hell are we at agreement . . ." (KJV). See Edmund Wilson, *Patriotic Gore: Studies in the Literature of the American Civil War* (New York: Oxford University Press, 1962), 91.
17. Genesis 49:11. E. A. Speiser corrects the translation of the tenseless Hebrew verb to the present and restores the poetic chiastic word order of the Hebrew: "In wine

he washes his garments / His robes in the blood of grapes" (*Genesis*, The Anchor Bible [Garden City, N.Y.: Doubleday, 1964]).

18. "The Valley of Decision" is the phrase Edith Wharton borrows from the prophet Joel for her historical novel about a historical social crisis (1902). Marcia Davenport also used it for a title.

19. Edward D. Snyder, "The Biblical Background of the Battle Hymn of the Republic," *New England Quarterly* 24, no. 2 (June 1951): 231–38. In this very short essay, Snyder surveys the biblical roots and cites (as well as the texts I have cited) Lam. 1:15, Isa. 13:9, and "grapes of gall" in Deut. 32:32.

20. Thomas Babington Macaulay, *Complete Writings . . . , Miscellanies* (Boston and New York: Houghton Mifflin, 1900), 3:291. It is Edmund Wilson who discovered the connection between this song and the "Battle Hymn" (*Patriotic Gore*, 93). Owen Dudley Edwards, one of the few to give Macaulay's verse anything like its due, writes that "Macaulay had intended that the crusading conviction of his bard would testify to the transformation of anti-Royalist arms from constitutional to social," and notes that the "Battle Hymn" in a similar manner marks the change "from a merely constitutional conflict into a crusade to emancipate the slaves" (*Macaulay* [London: Weidenfeld & Nicholson, 1988]), 13.

21. Boston and New York: Houghton Mifflin, 1900.

22. Christina Rossetti uses the figure in a poem, "The Three Enemies" (1851), which predates the "Battle Hymn" (1861). The Rossetti poem, however, is a poem of personal devotion, not a social statement: "Christ for my sake trod / The winepress of the wrath of God. . . . "

23. Thus the Geneva, Wisd. of Sol. 11:10; the KJV changes it slightly: "a groaning for the remembrance of things past" (11:11–12).

24. The work-in-progress translation by Richard Howard is called, much more accurately, *In Search of Lost Time*. See *Paris Review* 31, no. 111 (Summer 1989): 14–33.

25. *The Wisdom of Solomon*, trans. David Winston, Anchor Bible (Garden City, N.Y.: Doubleday, 1979), 225.

26. *Proverbs, Ecclesiastes*, trans. R. B. Y. Scott, Anchor Bible (Garden City, N.Y.: Doubleday, 1965), 209.

27. *Troilus and Criseyde* (1835–41), bk. 5, 11.

28. In the past century, John Henry Newman wrote, "I should dread to view it as literature. . . . " (Quoted in Matthew Arnold, *Unpublished Letters*, ed. Arnold Whitridge [New Haven: Yale University Press, 1923], 63); and recently James Kugel has shuddered, he says, to hear Joseph called "one of the most believable characters in Western literature," for Joseph, "is no *character* at all, but someone far more intimately ours," and he goes on to explain that the literary approach "puts the Bible on the wrong bookshelf." (*The Idea of Biblical Poetry: Parallelism and Its History* [New Haven and London: Yale University Press, 1981], 304).

29. Robert Alter and Frank Kermode, eds., *The Literary Guide to the Bible* (Cambridge, Mass.: Harvard University Press, 1987), 1–3.

30. Hans-Georg Gadamer, "On the Origins of Philosophical Hermeneutics," trans. Robert R. Sullivan, in *Philosophical Apprenticeships* (Cambridge, Mass. and London: MIT Press, 1985), 181. This essay originally appeared in German as *Philosophische Lehrjahre* (Frankfurt-am-Main: Vittorio Klostermann, 1977).

Chapter 2

1. This essay is a somewhat revised and shortened version of one published in *PMLA* 92, no. 5 (October 1977): 987–1004. In the intervening years the field has expanded wonderfully. See M. O'Connor, *Hebrew Verse Structure* (Winona Lake, Ind.: Eisenbrauns, 1980); James L. Kugel, *The Idea of Biblical Poetry: Parallelism and Its History* (New Haven and London: Yale University Press, 1981); Robert Alter, *The Art of Biblical Poetry* (New York: Basic Books, 1985); Adèle Berlin, *The Dynamics of Biblical Parallelism* (Bloomington: Indiana University Press, 1985); Harold Fisch, *Poetry with a Purpose: Biblical Poetics and Interpretation* (Bloomington: Indiana University Press, 1988). However, no one has really addressed my subject, or refuted my thesis. The standard old studies were George Buchanan Gray, *The Forms of Hebrew Poetry* (1915; reprint, with a Prolegomenon by D. N. Freedman, New York: Ktav Publishing House, 1972); Theodore H. Robinson, *The Poetry of the Old Testament* (London: Duckworth, 1947).

2. Gen. 11:6. All biblical references in this essay will be to the KJV unless otherwise noted.

3. (London: Oxford University Press, 1975), 244.

4. See, e.g., Thomas Fawcett, *The Symbolic Language of Religion* (London: SCM Press, 1970), esp. 273.

5. From the "Prospective" chapter of *Sartor Resartus*, bk. 1, in *The Works of Thomas Carlyle*, ed. H. D. Traill (London: Chapman and Hall, 1896–99), 1:57.

6. James Muilenburg, "Form Criticism and Beyond," *Journal of Biblical Literature* 88, pt. 1 (1969): 1–18.

7. *The Prison-House of Language* (Princeton: Princeton University Press, 1972), 127.

8. In *Near Eastern Studies in Honor of William Foxwell Albright*, ed. Hans Goedicke (Baltimore: Johns Hopkins University Press, 1971), 203. Oddly, Robert Alter says Psalm 137 virtually avoids semantic parallelism (*Art of Biblical Poetry*, 19).

9. With C. Franke Hyland, "Psalm 29: A Structural Analysis," *Harvard Theological Review* 66 (1973): 237.

10. *Patterns in the Early Poetry of Israel*, Studies in Ancient Oriental Civilization, no. 32 (Chicago: University of Chicago Press, 1963), 97.

11. "On Freedom in Poetry," in *Naked Poetry*, ed. Stephen Berg and Robert Mezey (Indianapolis: Bobbs-Merrill, 1969), 124.

12. Matthew Arnold writes in 1883 of the translatable qualities of OT verse:
    The effect of Hebrew poetry can be preserved and transferred in a foreign language, as the effect of other great poetry cannot. The effect of Homer, the effect of Dante, is and must be in great measure lost in translation, because their poetry is a poetry of metre, or of rhyme, or both; and the effect of these is not really transferable. A man may make a good English poem with the matter and thought of Homer and Dante, may even try to reproduce their metre, or to reproduce their rhyme; but the metre and the rhyme will be in truth his own, and the effect will be his, not the effect of Homer and Dante. Isaiah's, on the other hand, is a poetry, *as is well known, of parallelism* [my emphasis]; . . . the effect of this can be transferred to another language. . . .

"Isaiah of Jerusalem," in *The Complete Prose Works of Matthew Arnold*, ed. R. H. Super (Ann Arbor: University of Michigan Press, 1974), 10:102. See also, in "Religion Given," Arnold's explication of Job 28:28 on the basis of parallelism: " 'The fear of the Eternal' and 'To depart from evil' here mean, and are put to mean, and by the very laws of Hebrew composition which make the second phrase in a parallelism repeat the first in other words, they *must* mean, just the same thing" (6:193).

13. The following is condensed from Norman K. Gottwald's article s.v. "Poetry, Hebrew," in *The Interpreter's Dictionary of the Bible*, ed. George A. Buttrick (New York: Abingdon, 1962), vol. 3. For an excellent short survey, see Benjamin Hrushovski's article "Prosody, Hebrew," in the *Encyclopedia Judaica*.

14. Chapter 6 takes up Lowth and his criticism.

15. For a literary analysis of the text of Handel's *Messiah* see chapter 5.

16. Eugene A. Nida, "Principles of Translation as Exemplified by Bible Translating," in *On Translation*, ed. Reuben A. Brower (Cambridge, Mass.: Harvard University Press, 1959), 11–31.

17. "The force-not-ourselves" and "the stream-of-tendency" are Arnold's efforts to define "God" without metaphor and to reveal thereby Hebrew metaphor as metaphor, and "Israel" as a poet (*Complete Prose*, 6:181, 184, 190–91).

18. *The Enjoyment of Scripture* (New York: Oxford University Press, 1972), 192–93.

19. See, above all, Frank Kermode's memorable *Sense of an Ending* (New York: Oxford University Press, 1966).

20. *Le Livre de Job, traduit de l'hébreu, avec une étude sur l'âge et le caractère du poème*, 7th ed. (Paris: Calmann-Lévy, 1922). This book was well known to Arnold, and it was perhaps through it that he became familiar with the device of parallelism. Renan printed the parallel lines as such. He recognized the importance of parallelism for exegesis, defending an emendation with "sens conseillé par le parallélisme" (vi n). He writes:

La séparation des versets et des vers, qui est bien du fait de l'auteur, a été également maintenue. Le rhythme de la poésie hébraïque consistant uniquement dans la coupe symétrique des membres de la phrase, il m'a toujours semblé que la vraie manière de traduire les oeuvres poétiques des Hebreux était de conserver ce parallélisme, que nos procédés de versification, fondés sur la rime, la quantité, le compte rigoureux des syllabes, défigurent entièrement. J'ai donc fait tous mes efforts pour qu'on sentît dans ma traduction quelque chose de la cadence sonore qui donne tant de charme au texte hébreu. Il est certain que la métrique de ces vieilles poésies consistant uniquement en une sorte de *rime de pensées*, toute traduction soignée devrait rendre cette rime aussi bien qui l'original. (xi–xii)

21. Philip E. Lewis, "Merleau-Ponty and the Phenomenology of Language," in *Structuralism*, ed. Jacques Ehrmann (Garden City, N.Y.: Anchor-Doubleday, 1970), 17. This was originally a special issue of *Yale French Studies* (1966).

22. Jean Piaget has a convenient summary in *Le Structuralisme*, Que sais-je sér. no. 1311 (Paris: Presses Universitaires de France, 1974).

23. Ibid., 7. My translation.

24. *New Literary History* 4 (1973): 331–56. This was also published in French, in Staro-

binski, *Trois fureurs* (Paris: Gallimard, 1974), 73–126, a longer version of an essay previously published in *Analyse structurale et exégèse biblique,* ed. François Bovon (Neuchâtel, Switzerland: Delachaux et Niestlé, 1971), 63–94.

25. Perhaps the most famous case of doctrine influencing translation, however, is the passage from Isaiah, "Behold, a virgin shall conceive . . . " (7:14). The KJV translators were so absolutely confident that the passage predicts Christ's birth of Mary that, although the Hebrew word means simply "young woman," they wrote in all honesty "virgin." In this case, there is no "rhyming" line to help in exegesis.

26. Lévi-Strauss, "Overture" to *Le Cru et le cuit,* trans. J. H. McMahon, in *Structuralism,* 51–52.

27. A modest but valuable study in this challenging field is D. B. Fry's *Some Effects of Music,* the transcript of a lecture (Tunbridge Wells, England: Institute for Cultural Research, 1971). Fry is stronger on music and physics than on physiology, however. See also Lewis Thomas, "The Music of *This* Sphere," in *The Lives of a Cell* (New York: Viking, 1974), 20–25.

28. Lévi-Strauss, "Overture," 52.

29. This famous dictum of Pater's draws on a clue from Hegel. It occurs in Pater's essay "The School of Giorgione" (1888), in *The Renaissance* (Berkeley and Los Angeles: University of California Press, 1980), 106.

30. See Robert E. Ornstein, *The Psychology of Consciousness* (New York: Viking, 1972).

31. *Confessions of an Inquiring Spirit,* 3d ed. (1853; reprint, London: Adam and Charles Black, 1956), 42–43.

32. *Sermons of John Donne,* ed. G. R. Potter and E. M. Simpson (Berkeley and Los Angeles: University of California Press, 1953–63), 2:170–71.

33. Compare the correlations of structuralist "fonctions distributionelles," in François Bovon's Introductory Essay to *Analyse structurale et exégèse biblique,* 19.

Chapter 3

1. This essay in a short form was originally commissioned by the MLA for a collection, *Approaches to Teaching the Hebrew Bible as Literature in Translation,* ed. Barry N. Olshen and Yael S. Feldman (New York: MLA, 1989). It is expanded here to include some consideration of metaphor in the CB.

2. Kenneth Burke, "The First Three Chapters of Genesis," in *The Rhetoric of Religion: Studies in Logology* (Boston: Beacon, 1961), 201–7.

3. See, for instance, George Lakoff and Mark Johnson, *Metaphors We Live By* (Chicago: University of Chicago Press, 1980). One can go further and say with Fritz Mauthner that all language is essentially metaphorical. "Real truth is a metaphorical concept; men have reached the concept of truth, like the concept of God, without relying on experience. In this way it is possible to say that God is truth." Quoted in Linda Ben-Zvi, "Samuel Beckett, Fritz Mauthner, and the Limits of Language," *PMLA* 95, no. 2 (March 1980): 191.

4. It is very interesting that in China part of the Confucian canon is the *Book of Poetry,* some of which is as frankly erotic as the Song of Songs. The Chinese scholars' rationale for the canonization is strikingly parallel to that of the Song of Songs: the erotic poems are allegories of spiritual truths. In both cases the rationale has been

made with the most extravagant ingenuity. Finally, we need not deplore this ingenuity, for it is what has preserved for us these fine earthy texts. Zhang Longxi presents the parallels in "The Letter or the Spirit: The *Song of Songs*, Allegoresis, and the *Book of Poetry*," *Critical Inquiry* 39, no. 3 (Summer 1987): 193–217. Marvin H. Pope gives a history of the criticism in the Anchor Bible *Song of Songs* (Garden City, N.Y.: Doubleday, 1977), 17–210.

5. There is certainly at times a failure in communication, even in the Psalms. In Mendelssohn's *Elijah*, the chorus sings Psalm 84, "Wie lieblich sind deine Wohnungen" with great effect; but when *Elijah* is sung in English, the KJV has to be rejected as remarkably awkward and unsingable: "How amiable are thy tabernacles"! and the usual English singing version is changed to "How lovely is thy dwelling place." A. N. Wilson in his novel *A Bottle in the Smoke* (London: Sinclair-Stevenson, 1990) has a querulous old lady objecting—with reason—to the part of Psalm 119 that had been read at the service that morning: "*I am become like a bottle in the smoke*. Whatever would that mean?" (119:83). She also objects to saying she is "like a pelican in the wilderness" (102:6). The clergyman answers her objections with hopelessly desperate exegeses. (Dahood has for 119:83, "For I have become like one weeping from smoke," which makes some sense; and for 102:6 he has *vulture* instead of the rather comic *pelican*. *Psalms III*, Anchor Bible [Garden City, N.Y.: Doubleday, 1970]).

6. See Phyllis Trible, "Depatriarchalizing in Biblical Interpretation," *Journal of the American Academy of Religion* 41 (1973): 30–48.

7. W. D. Davies, "My Odyssey in New Testament Interpretation," *Bible Review* (June 1989): 10–18.

8. Noted by Frank Kermode, "Introduction to the New Testament," in *The Literary Guide to the Bible* (Cambridge, Mass.: Harvard University Press, 1987), 382.

9. *Matthew*, trans. W. F. Albright and C. S. Mann, Anchor Bible (Garden City, N.Y.: Doubleday, 1971), 84.

10. William A. Curtis, *Jesus Christ the Teacher* (London: Oxford University Press, 1943), 99, quoted in Leland Ryken, *The New Testament in Literary Criticism* (New York: Frederick Ungar, 1984), 157.

11. "English Translations of the Bible," in *The Literary Guide to the Bible*, 663.

12. Northrop Frye, *The Great Code: The Bible and Literature* (New York and London: Harcourt Brace Jovanovich, 1982), xiv.

13. For example, see Paul Ricoeur, *The Rule of Metaphor*, trans. Robert Czerny et al. (Toronto: Toronto University Press, 1977), 320–22.

Chapter 4

1. This is slightly altered from an essay originally published in *Language, Logic, and Genre: Papers from the Poetics and Literary Theory Section of the MLA*, ed. Wallace Martin (Lewisburg: Bucknell University Press, 1974), 28–43.

2. P. W. Bridgman, *The Way Things Are* (Cambridge, Mass.: Harvard University Press, 1959), 6.

3. J. Van Heijenoort, "Gödel," in *Macmillan Encyclopedia of Philosophy* (New York and London: Macmillan, 1967).

4. *Language and Mind* (New York: Harcourt Brace, 1968), 82–84.

5. *Way Things Are*, 7.
6. In this discussion of *Oedipus* I do not follow the Aristotelian tragic-flaw theory.
7. *A Grammar of Motives* (1945; reprint, Berkeley and Los Angeles: University of California Press, 1969), 512.
8. See "Quinque Viae," *Summa Theologica* 1:2–3.
9. It may be of interest to note that Anthony Trollope, whose art can also be called "ironic," especially loves "Scipio's Dream" and appends his own translation of it to his two-volume study of Cicero.
10. In "Lines Composed a Few Miles above Tintern Abbey" (1798) Wordsworth, who was quite enfranchised from all ecclesiastical orthodoxy, finds in his own carefully observed feelings a sort of religious experience:

> I have felt
> A presence that disturbs me with the joy,
> Of elevated thoughts; a sense sublime
> Of something far more deeply interfused,
> Whose dwelling is the light of setting suns,
> And the round ocean and the living air,
> And the blue sky, and in the mind of man:
> A motion and a spirit, that impels
> All thinking things, all objects of all thought,
> And rolls through all things.

(93–102)

11. Matthew Arnold, *The Complete Poems*, 2d ed., ed. Miriam Allott (London and New York: Longman, 1979), 154–206.
12. *Complete Prose*, 1:1.
13. See *Complete Poems*, 179 n.
14. *Works of Thomas Carlyle*, ed. H. D. Traill (London: Chapman and Hall, 1896–99), 5:108 (*Heroes and Hero-Worship*); 28:6 ("Characteristics"); 5:26 (*Heroes and Hero-Worship*).
15. *Works*, 28:27.
16. *Pensées*, no. 477.
17. *Notebooks 1914–1916*, trans. G. E. M. Anscombe (New York: Harper, 1961), 83.
18. *King Lear*, 5:17.
19. Ernest Nagel and James R. Newman, *Gödel's Proof* (New York: New York University Press, 1958), 98–102.
20. See his *Ideen zu einer reinen Phänomenologie und phänomenologischen Philosophie* (Halle, Germany: Niemeyer, 1913). Translated by W. R. Boyce Gibson as *Ideas—General Introduction to Pure Phenomenology* (London: George Allen and Unwin, 1931).
21. William Safire, for instance, has just published his richly meditated and witty book *The First Dissident: The Book of Job in Today's Politics* (New York: Random House, 1992).

Chapter 5

1. Christopher Hogwood, who is associated with chaste and scholarly performances, directed as a sort of *jeu d'esprit* an imitation of this Victorian performance in the Hollywood Bowl in 1985.

2. *Spectator,* no. 405, quoted in Murray Roston, *Prophet and Poet: The Bible and the Growth of Romanticism* (Evanston: Northwestern University Press, 1965), 53.

3. *Poems,* ed. John Butt (London: Methuen, 1963), 183–94.

4. *Times Literary Supplement,* July 26, 1991, 17.

5. See Philip Brett and George Haggerty, "Handel and the Sentimental: The Case of 'Athalia,'" *Music and Letters* 68, no. 2 (April 1987): 112–27. Brett and Haggerty explore in particular how Racine's austere and ironic drama is adapted in English to conform to the growing English taste for "sentimentalism," but they also describe this interesting early phase of the development of the English oratorio.

6. Robert Manson Myers has made a good study of its reception: *Handel's Messiah, A Touchstone of Taste* (New York: Macmillan, 1948; reprint, New York: Octagon Books, 1971).

7. *Handel's Dramatic Oratorios and Masques* (London: Oxford University Press, 1959), viii.

8. Ruth Smith, "The Achievements of Charles Jennens (1700–1773)," *Music and Letters* 70, no. 2 (May 1989): 161–89. This reference I owe to my colleague Philip Brett, who has helped me at many other points as well. Recent studies of Handel have given Jennens more credit than he used to get. H. C. Robbins Landon grants the *Messiah* libretto was "compiled with great sensitivity" (*Handel and His World* [London: Weidenfeld and Nicolson, 1984], 172). Christopher Hogwood finds Jennens self-important and opinionated but concedes that he had "taste and learning . . . [and] remarkable ability to construct the kind of libretto that suited Handel best," and notes the coherence of the whole "display of the divine scheme" (*Handel* [London: Thames and Hudson, 1984], 154, 168). Jonathan Keates detects in Jennens "a refined literary taste at work, allied to an intelligent awareness of Handel's own priorities as a musical dramatist" (*Handel and His Music* [London: Gollancz, 1985], 260).

9. Smith, "Achievements," 172.

10. Parts of Collins's *Discourse* are anthologized in the recent *Critics of the Bible 1724–1873,* ed. John Drury (Cambridge: Cambridge University Press, 1989).

11. Smith, "Achievements," 181.

12. Smith cites plentiful documentary evidence, e.g., 182.

13. Quoted in Smith, "Achievements," 183.

14. See Myers, *Handel's Messiah,* 69–73.

15. Smith, "Achievements," 187.

16. Ibid., 185.

17. The medieval French *Play of Daniel* exhibits this thoroughly, as the twentieth-century revival shows, in W. H. Auden's English version.

18. "The Text of 'Messiah'," *Music and Letters* 31, no. 3 (July 1950): 226–30. Cuming's indications of the liturgical connections are incorporated into my comments, and summarized here:

    Part I Mostly from the PB for Advent and Christmas.

        Isaiah 40:1–4 Quoted in the Gospel for fourth Sunday in Advent, and used in the Epistle for St. John the Baptist day (June 24).

        Haggai 2:6–7, Malachi 3:1–3 Connected by tradition to Isaiah 60.

        Isaiah 7:14 Christmas Day, Evensong.

Isaiah 40:9 Epistle for St. John the Baptist day.

Isaiah 60:1–3 Christmas Eve, Evensong.

Isaiah 9:2, 6; Luke 2:8–14 Christmas Day, Matins.

Zechariah 9:9–10, quoted in Luke 19:38 The Gospel for first Sunday in Advent.

Isaiah 35:5–6 Not liturgical. Quoted in Matthew 11:5.

Isaiah 40:11 Not liturgical. Suggested by John 10:14.

Matthew 11:28 The Comfortable Words of the Communion Service.

Part II Mostly from the PB for Easter.

John 1:29 Roman Catholic liturgy; Alternative Communion Service, PB. (Cuming missed this one.)

Isaiah 53:3, 4–6 Good Friday Evensong.

Isaiah 50:6 Epistle for Tuesday in Holy Week.

Psalm 22:7–8 Good Friday Matins.

Psalm 69:21 Good Friday Evensong.

Lamentations 1:12 Ancient custom of singing the "Reproaches" on Good Friday.

Isaiah 53:8 Good Friday Evensong.

Psalm 16:10, as quoted in Acts 2:27 Epistle for Easter Evensong.

Psalm 24:7–10 Ascension Day, Evensong.

Hebrews 1:5–6 Epistle for Christmas Day.

Psalm 68: 18, 11 Whitsun Matins.

Romans 10:15, quoting Isaiah 52:7 Not liturgical.

Romans 10:18, quoting Psalm 19:4 Not liturgical.

Psalm 2:1–4, 9 Easter Day Matins.

Revelation 19:6, 11:15, 19:16 Not liturgical.

Part III Mostly the Burial Service.

Job 19:25–26 Burial Service.

I Corinthians 15:20–22, 51–57 Easter Service, Burial Service.

Romans 8:31, 33–34 Not liturgical.

Revelation 5:12–13 Not liturgical.

Amen

19. In this case he chose Lamentations 1:4 for the great anthem, "The ways of Zion do mourn." Paul Henry Lang, *George Frideric Handel* (New York: W. W. Norton, 1966), 342 n.

20. Friedrich Chrysander, vol. 45 of *G. F. Händels Werke: Ausgabe der Deutschen Händelgesellschaft* (Leipzig, 1901; Farnborough, England: Gregg Press, 1966). Donald Burrows has recently brought out an "urtext edition" which collates eleven versions, 1742–54 (London, Frankfurt, and New York: Peters, 1987). There is an edition by J. M. Coopersmith (New York: Carl Fischer, 1947) that usefully compares the text with the KJV, noting omissions and changes. Coopersmith, however, is unaware of the PB and the Douay Version.

21. The problem is ingeniously faced in a new recording by Nicholas McGegan (Harmonia Mundi France HMU 907050/2, 1991; three CDs, two cassettes) in which you can adjust the sequences to achieve any of the versions. See Nicholas Kenyon, "*Messiah* Meets the Millennium," *New York Times*, Nov. 24, 1991, Arts sec., 29.

22. See Myers, *Handel's Messiah*, 104.

23. Quoted in Smith, "Achievements," 181.

24. Tenor in most performances. Burrows gives a chart (p. vi) showing Handel's own alternates.

25. See W. Jardine Grisbrooke, *Anglican Liturgies of the Seventeenth and Eighteenth Centuries* (London: S.P.C.K., 1958. Alcuin Club Collections, no. 40), 180, 294. Grisbrooke includes texts and discussion of two Nonjurors' Liturgies.

26. John Tobin believes that Jennens added the *Thy* to implicate the audience, but the *Thy* is right there in the PB. See "Vorwort" to *The Messiah*, Hallische Händel-Ausgabe, serie 1, band 17 (Basel: Bärenreiter Kassel, 1965), ix.

27. *Psalms II*, ed. and trans. Mitchell Dahood, Anchor Bible (Garden City, N.Y.: Doubleday, 1968), 133.

28. The oldest Douay (Doway, 1609) has *gentiles,* but the later ones changed to *nations* to represent Jerome's *gentes.*

29. See *Job,* ed. and trans. Marvin H. Pope, Anchor Bible (Garden City, N.Y.: Doubleday, 1965), 146.

30. Or treble in other versions. Burrows, v.

31. See, for instance, *Ritual Murder,* ed. Brian Morris (Manchester: Carcanet Press, 1980). C. H. Sisson writes:

    Everyone is caught in the decay of our speech, and the Church can only say what it has to say through language it has made its own. It was one of the great conquests of the sixteenth and seventeenth centuries that the Church commanded a language at once profound and familiar. Now, after immense deliberations, it injects trashy and unmeaningful speech even into the liturgy. There is no such thing as passing on profound truths in superficial speech. (Quoted in Morris, 123)

32. John Newton, rector of the Parish Church of St. Mary, Lombard Street, in London, who left his own mark on our culture by composing the words of the popular hymn "Amazing Grace," exploited Handel's *Messiah* for his evangelical ends. He had long wanted, he says, to preach a series of sermons encompassing the essential Christian message, and the immense popularity of *Messiah* in 1784 gave him the idea that the libretto would supply the framework for such a series, and accordingly he composed his "Fifty Sermons." To this devout evangelical, "The arrangement or series of passages is so judiciously disposed, so well connected, and so fully comprehends all the principal truths of the Gospel, that I shall not attempt either to alter or to enlarge it" (*Fifty Expository Discourses on the Series of Scriptural Passages, which form the subject of the celebrated Oratorio of Handel* [Philadelphia: Wm. W. Woodward, 1812], 1:4).

33. Quoted from Herder's *Briefe das Studium Theologie Betreffend* in Myers, *Handel's Messiah*, 270, 275. Klopstock had already done a translation in 1775. See Tobin, "Vorwort," ix. Klopstock's *Messias,* 1748–73, might occur to the reader as comparable with Handel's *Messiah,* but not so. It is a long epic inspired by *Paradise Lost,* covering the Passion and Resurrection, with imaginary amplifications. Matthew 27:52–53, for instance, expands to fill two cantos; Moses addresses Paul, Eve appears to the Virgin Mary, and so on.

34. As in the 1990 U.S. Harmonia Mundi recording, Nicholas McGegan, director.

35. *Letters of Edward Fitzgerald,* ed. A. M. Terhune and A. B. Terhune (Princeton: Princeton University Press, 1980), 1:424; 2:36.

36. See Dean, *Handel's Dramatic Oratorios and Masques,* 168, 169, 228 *et passim;* Lang, *Handel,* 211, 232 *et passim.*

37. *Letters,* 2:499.

38. Lang, *Handel,* 555.

39. Quoted in ibid., 556.

40. *The New Grove Handel* (New York and London: W. W. Norton, 1983), 25.

41. *New Grove Handel,* 110. Lang also refutes the "conversion theory" of Handel's life, at some length.

42. Quoted by Hamish Swanston in "Hallelujah Case-Study," *Times Literary Supplement,* March 29, 1991, 11.

43. *New Grove Handel,* 110–11.

Chapter 6

1. This is not "Orientalism" as Edward Said understands it, a racist condescension to inferior culture, but rather as devoted philological study and appreciation of the culture of the Near East.

2. See Brian Hepworth, *Robert Lowth* (Boston: Twayne, 1978). Murray Roston makes a very good study of Lowth in context in *Prophet and Poet: The Bible and the Growth of Romanticism* (Evanston: Northwestern University Press, 1965). Wordsworth rejects the "poetic diction" of the preceding age and declares for "the language really used by men" in his "Preface to Lyrical Ballads," 1802.

3. James L. Kugel, *The Idea of Biblical Poetry: Parallelism and Its History* (New Haven and London: Yale University Press, 1981). Kugel's learning is vast and fascinating.

4. Reprinted in 2 vols. (Hildesheim: Georg Olms Verlag, 1969).

5. Introduction by Vincent Freimarck, xxv. This Introduction is one of the best studies we have of Lowth.

6. Hans W. Frei complains that Lowth avoids the question of narrative truth in the Bible but neglects to note that Lowth's concern is the poetry. Frei's concern is narrative. *The Eclipse of Biblical Narrative* (New Haven and London: Yale University Press, 1974), 141–42.

7. Outside of the *Praelectiones,* he took the trouble to confute Bishop Hare's *System of Hebrew Metre* with withering scorn and relentless logic. The "Confutation" is published as an Appendix to the *Lectures.*

8. Roston, *Prophet and Poet,* 133.

9. This idea, however, is not borne out by Dahood's version. (*Psalms III,* trans. Mitchell Dahood, Anchor Bible [Garden City, N.Y.: Doubleday, 1970]).

10. Quoted in Freimarck, Introduction to *Lectures,* xiv.

11. See Hepworth, *Robert Lowth,* 194 n.

12. *Isaiah, A New Translation with a Preliminary Dissertation and Notes,* 2 vols. (London: J. Dodsley, 1778).

13. *Critics of the Bible 1724–1873* (Cambridge: Cambridge University Press, 1989), 196 n; Lowth, *Isaiah* 1:10. I have restored Lowth's capitalization. Drury's book is marred

by careless editing: Murray Roston's *Prophet and Poet* is listed as by Royston, my own *Arnold and God* as by Ruth Roberts. And there is no index.

14. Renan's *Le Livre de Job* (Paris: Calmann-Levy, 1922), vin, and Stanley Gevirtz, *Patterns in the Early Poetry of Israel*, (Chicago: University of Chicago Press, 1963), 97.

15. Quoted in A. C. Partridge, *English Biblical Translation* (London: André Deutsch, 1972), 37.

16. Blake apparently read this and transferred the concept to the Bible as the "Great Code of Art." See John C. Villalobos, "A Possible Source for William Blake's 'The Great Code of Art,'" *ELH*, September, 1988, 36–40.

17. Preface to his edition of Isaiah, in *Collected Prose Works*, ed. R. H. Super (Ann Arbor: University of Michigan Press, 1960–77), 10:124.

18. Arnold's own copy is now in the Armstrong Browning Library at Baylor University.

19. R. S. Cripps, "Two British Interpreters of the Old Testament: Robert Lowth and Samuel Lee," *Bulletin of the John Rylands Library, Manchester* 35, no. 2 (March 1953): 385–404.

20. See Magen Broshi, "Beware the Wiles of the Wanton Woman . . . ," *Biblical Archaeology Review* 9, no. 4 (July/August 1983): 54–56. Broshi, in translating one of the Dead Sea Scrolls, insists that *nidah*, usually translated as *pollution*, is really *menstruation* and occurs frequently in that sense.

21. *Second Isaiah, A New Translation with Introduction and Commentary*, trans. John L. McKenzie, Anchor Bible (Garden City, N.Y.: Doubleday, 1968). This is not one of the longer or more searching volumes of the Anchor Bible. We still await the volume on Isaiah 1–39.

22. This is all doubly interesting lately as part of the history of Iraq. In fact the reader after 1991 will enjoy Lowth's note on the conquering of the great river; he quotes Virgil, who, "to express the submission of some of the eastern countries to the Roman arms, says, that the waters of the Euphrates now flowed more humbly and gently: 'Euphrates ibat jam mollior undis.' AEn. viii.726" (2:69).

23. *Eclipse of Biblical Narrative*, 141.

24. George Buchanan Gray, for instance, in *The Forms of Hebrew Poetry* (London, 1915; reprint, New York: Ktav, 1972).

25. *Idea of Biblical Poetry*, 13.

26. Ibid., 304.

27. See, for a corrective, Francis Landy, "The Case of Kugel: Do We Find Ourselves When We Lose Ourselves in the Text?" *Comparative Criticism 5*, ed. E. S. Shaffer (Cambridge: Cambridge University Press, 1983), 305–16.

28. Robert Alter, *The Art of Biblical Poetry* (New York: Basic Books, 1985), 10. Adèle Berlin, *The Dynamics of Biblical Poetry* (Bloomington: Indiana University Press, 1985) takes up the classification question with good sense and good humor. Her book is a valuable study from a linguistics point of view.

29. *Dynamics of Biblical Poetry*, 6. She quotes Empson's *Seven Types of Ambiguity* (London: New Directions, 1947), 24–25.

30. Robert Alter, "The Characteristics of Ancient Hebrew Poetry," in *The Literary Guide*

to the Bible, ed. Robert Alter and Frank Kermode (Cambridge, Mass.: Harvard University Press, 1987), 611–24. See p. 619.

31. *Historism: The Rise of a New Historical Outlook,* trans. J. E. Anderson (London: Routledge and Kegan Paul, 1972), 206. English translation of *Die Entstehung des Historismus* (Munich, 1936).

32. *The Spirit of Hebrew Poetry,* trans. J. Marsh (Burlington, Vt.: E. Smith, 1832).

33. See Isaiah Berlin's magisterial *Vico and Herder* (London: Hogarth Press, 1976).

34. Alexander Altmann, *Moses Mendelssohn, a Biographical Study* (University, Ala.: University of Alabama Press, 1973), 412–13. Altmann's translation.

35. See Winton Dean, *The New Grove Handel* (New York and London: W. W. Norton, 1983), 40–41. Ruth Smith says it was the annual Oxford celebration, the Encaenia, "Achievements," 165.

Chapter 7

1. *Biographia Literaria* (1817; reprint, London: George Bell and Sons, 1905), chap. 17, 164. Wordsworth had rejected the stilted and artificial "poetic diction" of the eighteenth-century poets and made his manifesto for the "language really used by men" in the "Preface to Lyrical Ballads," 1802.

2. Just because the Bible has provided Western culture with so large a part of the "patrimony of human collectivity" (see chap. 1, n. 9), it is a major resource for humor. Dorothy Parker called her pet canary Onan; one remembers that Onan, to avoid impregnating Tamar, "spilled his seed upon the ground" (Gen. 38:9). Another example is the fine French poem about Lot and his daughters:

    Il but, il devint tendre,

    Et puis, il fut son gendre.

3. From "Rejoice in the Lamb," *Poems by Christopher Smart,* ed. with an introduction by Robert Brittain (Princeton: Princeton University Press, 1950), 106.

4. Ibid., 109.

5. Ibid., 118–20.

6. I am indebted to my colleague Robert Essick for pointing out these items.

7. From "The Marriage of Heaven and Hell," *Poems* (London: Longman, 1971), 112.

8. *Poems,* 468.

9. See chapter 1.

10. Introduction to *Milton, Poems,* 488.

11. See Gay Wilson Allen, *The New Walt Whitman Handbook* (New York: New York University Press, 1975), 215.

12. After various informal revised translations. See, for instance, Luther A. Weigle, "English Versions Since 1611," in *Cambridge History of the Bible* (Cambridge: Cambridge University Press, 1963), 3, 361–82.

13. *Dictionary of National Biography,* 11th ed.

14. *The Book of the Prophet Isaiah, a New English Translation* (New York: Dodd Mead; London: James Clarke; Stuttgart: Deutsche Verlags-Anstalt, 1898).

15. DNB.

16. *Complete Prose,* 5:251.

17. Ibid., 7:504.

18. Ibid., 505.

19. R. H. Super gives us both introductions, the whole text of the Isaiah, and the notes: ibid., 7:5–72; 10:100–130 and 259–447. I analyze this work at some length in *Arnold and God* (Berkeley, Los Angeles, London: University of California Press, 1983), 244ff.

20. See Alexander Altmann, *Moses Mendelssohn* (University, Ala.: University of Alabama Press, 1973), 501.

21. *Complete Prose*, 10:102.

22. Especially in *Literature and Dogma, God and the Bible,* and such essays as "A Psychological Parallel" and "A Comment on Christmas."

23. *Complete Prose*, 5:88.

24. The material on Housman here was in a somewhat different form from the Presidential Address at a meeting of the Philological Association of the Pacific Coast in 1985, and was published in *Pacific Coast Philology* 21, nos. 1–2 (November 1986): 7–19.

25. Norman Marlow's *A. E. Housman: Scholar and Poet* (London: Routledge and Kegan Paul, 1958) is by far the best study of "Influences," for its phenomenal learning and literary sense.

26. Marlow, *Housman: Scholar and Poet*, 149.

27. *Letters,* ed. Henry Maas (London: Rupert Hart-Davis, 1971), 328 (1933). See also 381.

28. *The Collected Poems of A. E. Housman* (London: Jonathan Cape, 1939), 236–38. Hereafter referred to as *Poems.*

29. Laurence Housman, *My Brother A. E. Housman* (New York: Charles Scribner's Sons, 1938), 114. Hereafter, "Laurence."

30. Richard Perceval Graves, *A. E. Housman: The Scholar-Poet* (London: Routledge and Kegan Paul, 1979), 187.

31. Laurence, 114–15.

32. Laurence, 115.

33. *Poems*, 178.

34. *Poems*, 72.

35. *Poems*, 107.

36. *Poems*, 108.

37. See his statement to Joan Thomson in Graves, *Housman: Scholar-Poet*, 243.

38. *Selected Prose,* ed. John Carter (Cambridge: Cambridge University Press, 1961), 19–20.

39. *Poems*, 89–90.

40. *Poems*, 165. "Trouble came" is another echo of Job (3:26).

41. *Letters*, 141.

42. *Poems*, 101.

43. *Poems*, 171.

44. *Poems*, 158.

45. *Poems*, 181.

46. *Poems*, 70.

47. *Poems*, 157.

48. *Poems*, 210. And of course, 14, 24, 25, 141, 211, etc.

49. *Poems*, 65.

50. *Poems*, 107.
51. *Poems*, 10.
52. *Poems*, 144.
53. *Poems*, 166.
54. *Poems*, 111.
55. Psalm 119:19. In "The Name and Nature of Poetry" he demonstrates with examples his preference for the BP Psalms (*Selected Prose*, 187).
56. Tom Burns Haber, *A. E. Housman* (New York: Twayne, 1967), app. 179–93. This table is flawed in that Haber does not take note of the Apocrypha, or the PB version of the Psalms as different from the KJV, and in that some of the items seem to be questionable. But in the main, it is fair enough to be significant.

    Grant Richards, in his *Housman 1897–1936* (New York: Oxford, 1942) appends some papers by G. B. A. Fletcher, which include some tables of "reminiscences" including some biblical ones, 399–400. Marlow's *Housman: Scholar and Poet* has a section on his use of the Bible that is informed and sound, 104–16.
57. Marlow notes four echoes from Ecclesiasticus, ignored by Haber, *Housman: Scholar and Poet*, 111.
58. *Nineteenth Century* 115 (February 1934): 243–56.
59. *Letters*, 356.
60. *Poems*, 72.
61. See Gordon Pitts, "Housman's 'Be Still, My Soul,'" *Victorian Poetry* 3 (Spring 1965): 137–38. It is, says Pitts, a German hymn of Katherina von Schlegel, translated by Jane Laurie Borthwick, whose collected hymns appeared in 1862.
62. *Oedipus Coloneus* 1211–48; *Poems*, 244–45.
63. Laurence, 253.
64. *Letters*, 37.
65. *Letters*, 158.
66. Marlow, *Housman: Scholar and Poet*, 136.
67. *Poems*, 99.
68. *Poems*, 47.
69. *Poems*, 48.
70. Gerard Manley Hopkins, *Poems*, 3d ed., ed. W. H. Gardner (New York and London: Oxford University Press, 1948), 28.
71. Psalms 33:3, 96:1, 98:1, 144:9, 149:1; Isaiah 42:10.
72. *Poems*, 25–27. The sources are, especially, Numbers 13–14 and Exodus 12–27.
73. *Poems*, 38.
74. *Poems*, 43–45.
75. *Poems*, 113.
76. *Poems*, 70.
77. I prefer this reading as being the most logical, and in accord with newspaper accounts of Texas oil discoveries Hopkins would have read about in the newspapers of the 1880s. See Michael Taylor, "Hopkins' God's Grandeur, 3–4," *Explicator* 25, no. 8 (April 1967): 68.
78. *Poems*, 70–71.
79. *Confessions of an Inquiring Spirit*, 3d ed. (1853; reprint, London: Adam and Charles Black, 1956), 42–43.

General Index

Abel, 46
Acrostic poems (alphabetic), 109, 137
Adam, 2
Addison, Joseph, 76
Agnostics, 144
Akkadian poetry, 24, 25
Alfred, King, 4
Allegory, 113
Allen, Gay Wilson, 177
Alter, Robert, 13, 130, 166, 167, 176
Altmann, Alexander, 178
American place names, 6
Anglicans, 80, 141, 143
Anne, Queen, 78
Anthropomorphism, 52
Anxiety of influence, 162
Apocrypha, 10, 121
Aquinas, Thomas, 66, 160
Arabic, 108, 121
Aramaic, 108, 136
Aratus, 122
Aristotle, 119
Arnold, Matthew, 15, 122, 140–42, 143, 147, 166, 167, 168, 171, 176, 177, 178; definitions of God, 33; *Empeddocles on Etna*, 68–72
Arthurian legend, 1
Atheism, 104, 143, 144; "High-Church atheist," 144
Auden, W. H., 17, 172

Babel, 12, 46; Tower of, 2, 3, 17
Bach, J. S., 99, 105
Ballads, 143

Barthes, Roland, 3, 165
"Battle Hymn of the Republic," 6–9. *See* Howe, Julia Ward
Bentham, Jeremy, 17
Ben-Zvi, Linda, 169
Bercovitch, Sacvan, 165
Berg, Stephen, 167
Bergson, Henri, 36
Berlin, Adèle, 131, 167
Berlin, Isaiah, 177
Bethel, 1, 4, 6
Bethesda, 6
Bible, historicity of, 108
Bible, Versions of: admired by Lowth, 120; Anchor, 10, 124, 125, 153, 166, 174, 175, 176; Douay, 95, 96, 158, 159, 174; Geneva, 6, 10; Good News, 59; Hebrew Prayer Book, 32; KJV, 12, 13, 24, 26, 27, 28, 35, 59, 84–98, 100, 102, 119, 122, 125, 152; Jerome (Vulgate), 6, 11, 13, 14, 20–21, 24, 31, 35, 119, 158–59; Jerusa-lem, English, 124; Jerusalem, French, 20, 21, 124; Luther, German, 5, 12, 14, 21–22, 30, 35; NEB, 10, 11, 29, 59, 121, 124, 153; NIV, 11; PB Psalter (Cover-dale), 76, 79, 82, 90, 94, 102, 151; Revi-sion of 1885, 139, 153; RSV, 12, 124; Septuagint, 14, 32, 120, 129; Tremellius (Protestant Latin), 6; Turkish, 31
"Bible as Literature," 12, 13
Bildad, 64
Bishop of London, 82
Blake, William, 5, 138–39, 143, 176, 177; "Jerusalem," 138–39

181

Empson, William, 131, 176
Epistles, 80
Essick, Robert, 177
Eucharist, 80, 157
Evangelicalism, 79
Everyman, 47
Ewald, Heinrich, 139
Exodus, the, 113

Fawcett, Thomas, 167
Feldman, Yael S., 169
Fertile Crescent, 15
Fisch, Harold, 167
Fitzgerald, Edward, 103–4, 145, 175
Fletcher, G. B. A., 179
Folk songs, 143
Fourfold exegesis, medieval, 47, 119
Freedman, David Noel, 23, 24, 167
Frei, Hans W., 129, 175
Freimarck, Vincent, 175
Fry, D. B., 169
Frye, Northrop, 59, 138, 170

Gadamer, Hans-Georg, 15, 16, 166
Gardner, W. H., 179
Garrison, William Lloyd, 7
Gaster, Theodore H., 24
George I, 78
Gesenius, H. F. W., 122, 141
Gevirtz, Stanley, 24, 35, 119
Gideons, 12
Giza, Great Pyramid at, 5
Gladstone, William Ewart, 140
Glastonbury, 1
God: disappearance of, 75; finger of, 2; metaphors for, 33, 51, 115; speaks Hebrew, 136
Gödel, Kurt, 14, 42, 61–73; his theorem described, 61
Goedicke, Hans, 167
Goethe, Johann Wolfgang, 2, 52, 102
Goldsmith, Oliver, 143
Goshen, 6
Gospels, 80
Göttingen, 139
Gottwald, Norman K., 25, 168

Graves, Richard Percevel, 178
Gray, George Buchanan, 167, 176
Gray, Thomas, 143
Greek Anthology, 142
Greek language: hypotactic, 34; *Koine*, 14
Gregory, G., trans. Lowth's *Praelectiones*, 108
Grisbrooke, W. Jardine, 174
Grotius, Hugo, 121
Gutenberg, 2

Haber, Tom Burns, 179
Hades, 121, 127
Haggerty, George, 172
Hammond, Gerald, 59
Handel, George Frideric, 15, 26, 75–106, 133–34, 135, 139, 168; comes to England, 78; his Englishness, 103–4; his religious views, 104–6; works: *Acis and Galatea*, 78; *Alexander Balus*, 80; *Alexander's Feast*, 79; *Athalia*, 79, 105; *L'Allegro (and Il Penseroso and Il Moderato)*, 79; *Belshazzar*, 79, 82; *Deborah*, 79; *Deidamia*, 79; *Esther*, 78–79; *Hercules*, 79, 133; *Imaneo*, 79; *Jeptha*, 80, 105; *Joseph and his Brethren*, 79; *Joshua*, 79; *Judas Maccabeus*, 77, 79; *Messiah*, 15, 75–106; *Ode for St. Cecilia's Day*, 79; *Samson*, 79; *Saul*, 79, 81, 82; *Solomon*, 80; *Susanna*, 80, 103; *Theodora*, 105
Hare, Francis, 175
Hebrew language, 5, 13, 33
Hebrew poetry, 17–44, 76, 100, 117; biblical books in poetry; 25; paratactic poetic style, 34
Heijenoort, J. Van, 170
Heine, Heinrich, 143, 155
Hepworth, Brian, 175
Herbert, George, 160, 161
Hercules, 133–34
Herder, Johann Gottfried von, 102–3, 130, 131–32, 136, 174, 177
Higher Criticism, 15, 139
Hoadley, Benjamin, Bp., 108
Hogwood, Christopher, 104, 171, 172
Holy Grail, 1

Homer, 113, 121, 127, 141

Hopkins, Gerard Manley, 15, 154, 156–
62, 179; life: Roman Catholic convert,
Jesuit, 156; poems: "Barnfloor and
Winepress," 158; "God's Grandeur,"
160; "He hath abolished the old
drought," 156; "Nondum," 158; "A Soliloquy of One of the Spies Left in the
Wilderness," 157; "Starlit Night," 161;
"Thou art indeed just, Lord," 159

Horace, 17, 37, 121, 123, 135, 142, 143, 155

Housman, A. E., 15, 142–56; 178–79; life:
mother dies on his birthday, 145; religious views, 143–46; Professor of Latin,
Cambridge, 142; at University College,
London, 145; poems: "As I gird on for
fighting," 155; "Be still, my soul, be
still," 151; "The Carpenter's Son," 148–
49; "Easter Hymn," 149; "Epitaph on
an Army of Mercenaries," 150; "For My
Funeral," 149; "Ho, every one that
thirsteth," 148; "Illic Jacet," 147; "The
Immortal Part," 150; "Jubilee," 150;
"The laws of God," 150; "On Wenlock
Edge," 155; "Others, I am not the first,"
155; "What man is he," 153; "When Israel out of Egypt," 147

Housman, Lawrence (brother of A. E.),
143, 154, 178

Howard, Richard, 166

Howe, Julia Ward, 6–9

Hrushovski, Benjamin, 168

Hunt, Thomas, 121

Husserl, E. G. A., 72, 171

Hyland, C. Franke, 167

Hyphology, 3

Hypotaxis, 34

Inclusio, or Ring-Structure, 18, 19

Inspiration, 116

Intertextuality, 3, 4, 43, 142, 154

Isaiah, 15; Arnold's version, 140–42;
Cheyne's version, 139, 141; Handel's *Messiah* and, 83–93, 99;
Hopkins' use of, 161; Housman's
use of, 148; Gesenius' edition, 122,

141; Isaiah 14 illustrated by Blake,
138; Isaiah interpreted to predict
Jesus, 99, 125–27, 139, 141;
Lowth's translation, 118–29

Isomorphisms: Dan/Beersheba, Gath/
Eskalon, Judah/Israel, Sodom/Gomor-
rah, 42, 110

Italics in KJV, 14

Jacob, 1, 2, 7

James I of England, 4

James, William, 112

Jameson, Fredric, 23

Jennens, Charles, 77, 78, 79, 80–82, 83–
106

Jephthah, 2

Jeremiah, 142

Jerome. *See* Bible, Versions of

Jerusalem, 6; "Jerusalem," 138–39. *See*
Blake, William

Jesus, 8, 13, 15, 43, 54, 55–59; applies
prophecies of Isaiah to himself, 99;
prophesied in HB, 81, 86, 99, 125–27,
139, 141; prophesied by Virgil, 83;
speaks Aramaic, 136; uses metaphor,
55–59; uses parallelism, 123

Jews, 140, 141

Job, 14, 62–74, 137; compared to *Oedipus*,
117

John the Baptist, 84

Johnson, Mark, 169

Johnson, Samuel, 78, 143

Jones, William, 131

Joseph, 166

Joseph of Arimathea, 1

Josephus, 127

Judah, 7

Kalisch, Marcus, 140

Kant, Immanuel, 117

Keates, Jonathan, 172

Keats, John, 73, 143

Kennicott, Benjamin, 119

Kenyon, Nicholas, 173

Kermode, Frank, 13, 166, 168, 170

Bible Index